An Introduction to Data Handling in BBC BASIC

James Gatenby

Edward Arnold

© James Gatenby 1987

First published in Great Britain 1987 by
Edward Arnold (Publishers) Ltd
41 Bedford Square,
London WC1B 3DQ

Edward Arnold (Australia) Pty Ltd
80 Waverley Road
Caulfield East,
Victoria 3145
Australia

Edward Arnold
3 East Read Street,
Baltimore
Maryland 21202
USA

All rights reserved. No part of this publication may be reproduced, stored in a retrieval system, or transmitted in any form or by any means, electronic, mechanical, photocopying, recording, or otherwise, without the prior permission of Edward Arnold (Publishers) Ltd.

British Library Cataloguing in Publication Data

Gatenby, James
  An introduction to data handling in
BBC Basic.
  1. Electron Microcomputer—
Programming 2. BASIC (Computer
Program language)
  I. Title
  005.2'65   QA76.8.E38

ISBN 0-7131-3585-9

Text set in 10/11pt Times Compugraphic
by Mathematical Composition Setters Ltd., Salisbury, Wiltshire
Printed in Great Britain by The Alden Press, Oxford

Preface

The BBC Micro has established a dominant position as the leading educational computer in the United Kingdom. The language used, BBC BASIC, is superior to that provided on many machines and enables programs to be written easily in a style which is meaningful to the reader. BBC BASIC is also available on the Acorn Electron, so that the two machines embrace the computer language which most children use at school and which many college students require in their studies.

The Acorn Master Series uses BBC BASIC throughout the range from the Master 128 and Master Compact with 128K memory to the ultra-fast Master Scientific, used mainly in research. BBC BASIC is also used on the Master 512; this machine is compatible with the universal standard for business machines and has similar features to the IBM Personal Computers (PCs). The Acorn range of computers is designed to be 'upward compatible'— so programming techniques in BBC BASIC learned on the small machines such as the Electron and the BBC Model B will still be relevant on the most powerful business and scientific models.

This book concentrates on **Data Handling**, which really means the processing of raw facts to produce useful information. The subject covers all sorts of business, domestic and administrative activities from the keeping of personnel lists to commercial stock and sales records. It is probably true to say that data handling by computer can replace all similar activities which are currently done using paper and ink; it is certain that most commercial employment in the future will require some familiarity with the subject.

While it is expected that the reader of this book may have done some very elementary programming, the ideas are explained in simple, non-technical language intended for the beginner. Each idea is demonstrated with a clear, straightforward example and there is absolutely no complex mathematical work.

The aims of this book are as follows:

- To introduce structured BASIC programming leading on to serious data handling with random access files.
- To show that computer programming is not the exclusive domain of electronics and mathematics specialists — rather it involves the learning of the rules of a simple language similar to English.
- To demonstrate that programming may be simplified by drawing upon a library of standard 'modules'. These are independent procedures which may be utilised with little or no modification in a variety of different applications.

Computing jargon is a curse to the non-specialist user such as the owner of a small business: throughout this book such language has been avoided where possible and where it is unavoidable it has been explained. Each set of new ideas culminates in a simple program which incorporates and illustrates them. It is intended that these 'skeleton' programs will provide the user with a framework on which to build larger programs tailored to suit his or her individual needs.

After working through the book the reader should be able to produce complete 'menu-driven' programs to handle all types of records and be familiar with the creation and maintenance of random access data files on disk.

This work is particularly intended for:

- The student preparing for examination in Computer Studies, Data Processing and Computer Literacy.
- The home user wishing to streamline records on sport, collections, clubs and similar activities.
- The administrator in a large organisation such as a school, college, or hospital, who frequently needs to update personnel records, mailing lists, etc.
- The small business user wishing to automate records such as stock control, sales and accounting.

J. Gatenby
1986

Contents

Preface	3
1 Introduction	7
Program design	8
Modular design	9
Menu-driven programs	9
2 Entering Data	11
Meaningful variable names	11
Entering large quantities of data	11
Assigning DATA to subscripted variable stores—arrays	13
The DATA statements	14
Other methods of entering data	16
Summary	17
3 Screen Display	18
User control over the screen display	19
Introducing PROCEDURES	20
4 Searching	22
Searching for partial names	27
Searching for records satisfying more than one criterion	30
Searching for records within a certain numerical range	31
Summary	32
Revision of some ideas on structure	32
5 Menus and Procedures	33
The MENU	34
Entering the option	35
Extending the program	39
Global and local variables	41
Summary	43
6 Sorting Data	44
Speeding up the sort process—integer variables	51
Ever-decreasing looping	52

6 *Contents*

	The Shell sort	55
	Comparing the Bubble and Shell sorts	59
	Summary	60
7	**Developing a Menu-driven Program**	61
8	**Developing a General Purpose Data Handling Program**	68
	Using the program	74
	Searching on only one field	75
9	**Data Files**	76
	Sequential and random access files	80
	Sequential files	80
	Reading a file from disk to memory	81
	Developing a complete program	82
	Handling a very large file	88
10	**Random Access Files**	93
	Modifying a single field on the disk, using OPENUP	97
	Creating the file—moving the pointer	102
	Summary	103
11	**Towards a Viable Data Base Program**	104
	Introduction	104
	The record format	105
	File size	108
	The complete program	110
	The program in detail	112
	Suggestions for further work	118

Appendix 1 A Glossary of Terms used in Data Handling with BBC Microcomputers   120

Appendix 2 Graphical Presentation of Data   129
    1 The line graph   129
       The program in detail   133
    2 The bar chart   136
    3 The pie chart   138
    Summary   143

Index   145

1

Introduction

The microcomputers available today are quite capable of serious data processing in addition to their familiar role in the home as games machines and teaching aids. With the availability of relatively inexpensive disk drives and printers, the BBC Micro is easily expanded into a complete 'data processing' system; such a system will allow the serious user to carry out all of the main tasks concerned with the efficient storage and retrieval of data.

Four further developments provide the opportunity for the family of Acorn/BBC microcomputers to be used as part of a very powerful data processing system:

- The 'hard disk' allowing the storage of massive quantities of data.
- The creation of a 'network' linking a large number of micros together to enable the sharing of printers and storage facilities.
- The modem: a device which allows a microcomputer to be used for sending and receiving data over long distances via the telephone lines—giving access to national and international 'data bases' held in mainframe computers.
- The arrival of the BBC Master Series introduced a range of business-standard microcomputers and their increased memory sizes make possible the handling of large and very useful files of data. The Master 128 is sold with two 'bundled' packages included—a word processor for the production and editing of text, and a spreadsheet for manipulation of table figures. These two aspects of computing, together with 'data handling' introduced in this book, form the core of modern office automation.

At this stage it may be appropriate to attempt to define what is meant by the terms 'data handling' or 'data processing'. The handling of records by manual methods has existed since the Domesday Book and before: now the term data processing really applies to handling records using electronic devices. (It is quite feasible to carry out this work with no knowledge of the electronic devices which form part or all of the data processing system).

Many people who could quite easily cope with electronic data processing are put off because they mistakenly believe the subject requires a high level of mathematical ability. While it is true that the early computers were used for 'number crunching', this is most definitely not the case nowadays. Increasingly the computer is used as a system for the storage and retrieval of data in the form of **text** rather than numbers, with facilities to **search** and **sort** far more efficiently than manual methods allow.

Data is really any type of raw facts which may be collected, from various sources, such as sporting records and statistics, vehicle performance details, a stock file or product catalogue in a small business, or details on hobbies such as gardening, cooking or music.

8   *Introduction*

The **processing** consists of converting the raw facts into useful information and this may involve:

- sorting (e.g. into alphabetical order)
- calculating (e.g. VAT, wages, etc.)
- searching (to find particular records).

When the processing is complete the information must then be **output** in a form meaningful to the user. The output medium may be the television/monitor screen, or it may be in the form of printed 'hard copy' on paper.

The three main phases of data processing are shown in Fig. 1.1.

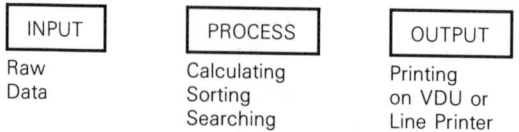

Fig. 1.1   The three stages of data processing

In addition, since it is necessary to retain data and information for future use it is essential to have a form of permanent **backing storage**. This consists of a magnetic storage medium such as cassette tape or floppy disk.

A minimal data handling system would therefore consist of the microcomputer, VDU (screen) and cassette recorder. For really serious work it would also be necessary to have a floppy disk drive and a line printer.

Of course, the owner of a BBC Micro or Acorn Electron can learn the essential skills of data handling using the basic system of micro plus cassette unit and eventually acquire the additional equipment as circumstances allow.

The modular design of the Master Series permits the user to progress upwards from the standard Master 128 machine; easily fitted devices convert the basic machine into any one of several high powered computers, while still retaining BBC BASIC and compatibility with the existing peripheral devices such as disk drives and printers.

Many computer owners start off by playing computer games that other people have written. Some computer owners may write their own games and find this exciting and challenging work. Data processing, on the other hand, can be just as rewarding and probably requires less inspiration or brilliant design. It is certainly very satisfying to see a computer turning out useful results from a program which you have written.

Program design

In this book we will concentrate on program planning and design, with the intention of producing **structured** programs. Structured programs have a clear layout which is easy to follow by a person other than the programmer.

Most of us, when we started programming, wrote the usual two line programs like:

```
10 PRINT"MY NAME"
20 GOTO 10
```

Of course, our initial aim was probably to see the computer produce something. Further effort produced larger programs which were an expansion of these crude ideas. The programs, entered directly at the keyboard, simply grew until they achieved the desired result.

Unfortunately this trial and error method of programming at the keyboard has several disadvantages:

- Programs are produced which are incomprehensible to other people and possibly also to the originator.
- It is slow and inefficient and if the equipment is shared it is also selfish.
- The program itself will probably be inefficient in its execution.
- It will be very difficult to modify or expand the program at some time in the future.

Modular design

In structured programming the intention is to produce a program which is easy to read and understand. The planning of the program consists of considering the main phases in the overall process without, at this stage, considering the minor details.

As an example, let us assume we want to read a set of data, carry out a process such as calculating or sorting, and display the results. The program falls naturally into three clearly defined blocks or modules as shown in Fig. 1.2.

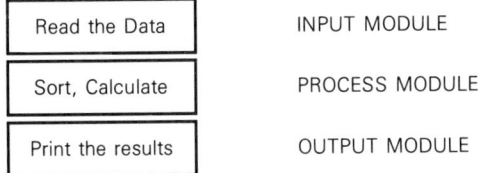

Figure 1.2

This may be an over-simplification of the planning of a program, but the general idea is that we start off with the broad outline and then fill in the details afterwards. This method is known as 'top down' programming.

Although we will all continue to enter small programs directly at the keyboard, it is suggested that the following strategy may be used for planning larger ones. Tear yourself away from the machine, and using pencil and paper (and rubber)—

- Block in the main modules of the program,
- Convert the modules to BASIC code,
- Carry out a 'dry-run' (a test with sample data, still using pencil and paper).

Now using the keyboard:

- Type in the program and *save* it *before* running.
  (It is always advisable to save text before running, since a 'crash' will necessitate retyping the whole lot).
- RUN the program.
- Carry out any necessary modifications and development.
- Save the program permanently on disk or cassette.

Menu-driven programs

Using the idea of program modules, programming becomes much simpler. Since data processing generally involves the same basic operations, such as sorting or searching, once we have written suitable modules which work we can use them again for future programs. Programming then becomes simply the selection and assembly of suitable well-tried modules, rather than writing the entire program from scratch, line by line. The version of the BASIC language used on the BBC Micro and Acorn Electron is particularly suitable for this approach, with amongst other things, the PROCEDURE facility.

A program can then consist of a set of independent modules written as PROCEDURES. These modules can be called up whenever necessary, so that we only run those parts of a program which we need at a particular time. The modules are selected from a **menu**, and after carrying out the required procedure, control is returned to the menu to allow a further selection to be made. The modules for a simplified menu-driven program are shown in Fig. 1.3.

```
    MENU
1 Read Data
2 Display
3 Search
4 End
```

```
READ DATA
```

```
DISPLAY
```

```
SEARCH
```

Fig. 1.3 The organisation of a simple modular program using PROCEDURES

One of the main aims of structured programming must be to make programs easier to follow. Unless memory capacity is a severe limitation, it is better not to have too many multiple-statement lines and it also makes for better reading if spaces are inserted fairly generously. High level languages like BASIC are supposed to be easy for humans to understand, but some of the listings appearing in magazines are exceedingly obscure. With the advent of machines such as the Master Series with much larger memories, the case for well-written programs with generous spacing becomes even stronger.

This introduction has discussed, in general terms, some of the arguments for planning and structure in data processing. The next chapters will attempt to show with simple examples how these ideas may be applied to practical programs. Very little knowledge of BASIC programming is required as the work starts at an elementary level, but it is assumed for instance, that the reader is familiar with the operation of the computer and may have written very simple programs.

By the end of this book you should be able to write substantial programs to create large files of data, which may be displayed, sorted or searched to find particular records, altered or amended to keep up-to-date. Such a file might be the personal details of the membership of a club, a company staff list, or a personal bank account.

2

Entering Data

Meaningful variable names

Consider the following program

```
10 READ A$,B
20 PRINT"NAME",A$
30 PRINT"AGE",B
40 DATA JOHN SMITH,32
50 END
```

Fig. 2.1 Meaningless variable names

Although this is a very simple example, it is not immediately clear that A$ is the string store used for name and B is the numeric store used to hold the age.

Using meaningful variable names, this elementary program would become:

```
10 READ name$,age
20 PRINT "NAME",name$
30 PRINT"AGE",age
40 DATA JOHN SMITH,32
50 END
```

Fig. 2.2 Meaningful variable names

There is no limitation on the length of a variable name, but obviously there is no point in exceeding the length necessary to remind potential users of the contents of the store. The use of such variable names will also reduce the need for REM statements to define every variable used.

Entering large quantities of data

REPEAT ... UNTIL
FOR ... NEXT

Let us assume we wish to enter 200 names and telephone numbers into the memory. We will use the variables *name$* and *phone$* respectively. With such a large amount of data it will be necessary to DIMension arrays *name$(I%)* and *phone$(I%)* as follows, allowing extra memory locations for expansion.

```
100 DIM name$(250),phone$(250)
```

12 Entering data

If we aim to create a flexible file of numbers which can be extended, if necessary, we may not have a known number of records to read in. However, we can overcome this by marking the end of the data with a record consisting of special 'dummy data'. This is then tested for in a REPEAT ... UNTIL loop.

```
10   DIM name$(250),phone$(250)
20   I%=0
30   REPEAT
40     I%=I%+1
50     READ name$(I%),phone$(I%)
60   UNTIL name$(I%)="***"
70
80   FOR N%= 1 TO I%-1
90     PRINT name$(N%),phone$(N%)
100    NEXT N%
110
120  DATA JOHN BROWN,4592
130  DATA MIKE SMITH,6848
140  DATA JILL GREEN,3721
150  DATA ***,***
```

Fig. 2.3

This is not a complete or useful program but it should illustrate a few important points relevant to structured programs.

1   Three distinct blocks of the program emerge, namely

```
┌─────────────────────────┐
│ Read the Data and       │
│ Assign to Variable      │
│ Array Stores            │
└─────────────────────────┘

┌─────────────────────────┐
│ Print the Records       │
└─────────────────────────┘

┌─────────────────────────┐
│ Data Statements         │
└─────────────────────────┘
```

Fig. 2.4

2 As the number of records to be read in may not be known, the reading cannot be done in a FOR ... NEXT loop, which requires a specified value to end the loop.
3 The REPEAT ... UNTIL loop, although slower than FOR ... NEXT, allows the testing for the end of DATA marker "***".
4 The use of the integer variable I% instead of the floating point variable I, as the subscript, greatly speeds the program. However, in future parts of this book, for the sake of clarity of presentation, integer variables will not be used. It is left as a task for the reader to insert integer variables wherever speed is essential.

When using REPEAT ... UNTIL it is important to make sure that the line I% = I% + 1 comes *before* the READ statement. Let us assume that we put the line at line 55 instead of line 40. Suppose there were 100 records in the DATA including the dummy record. After reading in the DATA, name$(100) would contain our dummy ***. If we now increment I% to I% + 1, then I% would be 101 and the text at line 60 would become, in effect

```
60 UNTIL name$(101) = "***"
```

Since this would not be true the condition for terminating the loop would never be satisfied.

This problem is avoided by including the line I% = I% + 1 *before* the READ statement.

When this program is entered and RUN, at the end of the READ module the counter I% has the value 4 and so name$(4) contains the 'dummy' data "***". Obviously this is not wanted, so when the display FOR ... NEXT loop is set up, it is necessary to print to I% − 1 to avoid printing the dummy data. So the FOR ... NEXT loop is actually set up to increment from N% = 1 to N% = 3 in this simple program. Note however that on completion of the FOR ... NEXT loop at line 100 N% will contain the value 4, not 3, and this may need to be allowed for in future expansion of the program.

Assigning DATA to subscripted variable stores — arrays

The use of subscripted variables allows all names, say, to be assigned to a variable store with the title *name$*. With the DATA as shown in Fig. 2.3 the file could be represented diagrammatically as follows:

Record No.	name$( )	phone$( )
1	JOHN BROWN	4592
2	MIKE SMITH	6848
3	JILL GREEN	3721
..	....	....

If we had 100 records, *name$*(1), *name$*(2) through to *name$*(100) would form one array, and *phone$*(1) to *phone$*(100) would form the second array.

Before the program is run, the DATA exists only in the DATA statements. During program execution, the READ statement assigns each **field** to the appropriate variable store. So that after running, Record 2 will be stored as follows:

name$(2) will contain MIKE SMITH
phone$(2) will contain 6848

Similarly, if we are using 100 records, the last record will be stored in *name$*(100) and *phone$*(100).

Once the DATA has been read into the arrays *name$*(·) and *phone$*( ) it may be manipulated easily. We could, for instance, check the contents of record 55 by entering in immediate mode (i.e. without a line number).

```
PRINT name$(55),phone$(55)
```

On pressing RETURN, the 55th fields in each of the two arrays will be displayed.

The main advantages of using subscripted variables as stores, however, are as follows:

1. Hundreds of items may be stored using only one variable name.
2. Once stored in the arrays, data may be processed in a FOR ... NEXT or REPEAT ... UNTIL loop without further reading. This is particularly useful for printing, searching, sorting or calculating operations on large arrays of DATA.
3. In data processing, the subscript forms a convenient Record No., useful for identifying records for amendment or deletion etc.

14 *Entering data*

Supposing we have assigned the name MIKE SMITH to store *name$(2)* and 6848 to store *phone$(2)* during the READ loop.

The contents of these stores will remain the same unless:

- The machine is switched off or NEW is entered.
- New data is assigned to the stores during the program execution.

Changing the contents of the stores in an array is necessary during the alphabetical sort routine (to be discussed later). This might be done using a statement such as

```
500 LET name$(I%)=name$(I%+1)
```

This means 'let store *name$(I%)* now contain a copy of the contents of store *name$(I% + 1)*'. In this case the original contents of store *name$(I%)* are **overwritten** by the contents of store *name$(I% + 1)*. Line 500 would not alter the contents of store *name$(I% + 1)*—the contents are only **copied** not transferred.

Clarity of presentation

To improve the general readability of the program in Fig. 2.3 blank lines have been inserted (lines 70 to 110) to separate the main modules of the program. This is achieved by typing the line number, then pressing the space bar, followed by RETURN. The command LISTO7 has also been used to cause indentation of the FOR ... NEXT and REPEAT ... UNTIL loops and to give spaces between the line numbers and the text.

Lower case and upper case letters

The use of lower case letters for variable names enables the reader of a program to distinguish between the variable names and the BASIC statements, which must be in capitals. It must be noted, however, that the lower case version *phone$*, for example, is treated as different from the upper case *PHONE$*. This must be allowed for in any search or sorting process if data involves a mixture of upper and lower case letters. I prefer to use lower case variable names, since any upper case name containing a BASIC reserved word will cause problems. For example, *MODEL$* will cause an error since it contains the BASIC keyword *MODE*. The use of the lower case i.e. *model$*, overcomes the problem.

The DATA statements

BBC BASIC allows much longer data statements than those shown in Fig. 2.3, and again these can be used when space is at a premium. However, a DATA statement of the maximum permissible length of 255 characters may be very difficult to read. This is particularly important when large quantities of data, perhaps containing a mixture of string and numeric fields, is entered. Any comma which is missed will cause data fields to be concatenated (stuck together) and the data will no longer be compatible with the requirements of the corresponding read statement.

To illustrate this consider a block of data relating to stock in a small business. The whole stock list is known as a **file**. Each product is known as a **record**, and individual pieces of data relating to this product are known as **fields**.

The DATA statements

	DESCRIPTION	NUMBER IN STOCK	UNIT COST PRICE
RECORD 1	TABLE	6	£150
RECORD 2	CHAIR	32	£ 25
RECORD 3	WINE-TABLE	5	£ 18
RECORD 4	SETTEE	1	£300
RECORD 5	BUREAU	3	£250

Fig. 2.5

The simplified block of data in Fig. 2.5 represents a file of stock in a furniture shop. A practical program would be to keep an up-to-date record of the stock, and possibly calculate total stock value, sales price after a mark-up of 20%, and add VAT at the current rate. The actual calculating processes are covered later in this book, and at this stage we will only concern ourselves with the entry of data. In BBC BASIC it would be quite feasible to enter this data in a single DATA statement as follows:

```
1000 DATA TABLE,6,£150,CHAIR,32,£25,WINE
-TABLE,5,£18,SETTEE,1,£300,BUREAU,3,£250
```

Fig. 2.6 An obscure DATA statement

Even longer statements than the above are permissible up to a maximum of 255 characters, and a realistic file would contain much more data.

One of the most common problems is that the data needs to be checked for compatibility with a READ statement such as

```
200   READ desc$(I),stock(I),cost$(I)
```

In practice, the variable list may be much longer so the process of checking for errors becomes even more difficult. Any missed comma or field will wreck the entire program.

Consider the more generous layout of the data below. Admittedly this is less economical on space, but if space is not a limitation, the ease of checking makes it worthwhile.

```
1000 DATA TABLE,6,£1.50
1010 DATA CHAIR,32,£25
1020 DATA WINE-TABLE,5,£18
1030 DATA SETTEE,1,£300
1040 DATA BUREAU,3,£250
```

Fig. 2.7 Separate DATA statements for each record

As each record occupies a separate line, it is easier to check for mistakes than the previous version. It would also be considerably simpler to modify the file by altering, inserting or deleting records.

Note that if we want to do any calculation on the prices, we must not store the price in string store *cost$*. Since the contents of string stores cannot be treated as mathematical numbers (only as individual separate characters like a car registration number) we cannot multiply or divide etc. We must either store the price (without the £ sign) in a numeric store, e.g. *cost*, or convert the contents of *cost$* to a number using VAL. At this stage the former is the simplest option.

Other methods of entering data

READ and DATA statements are not the only methods of putting data into the memory.

The INPUT statement allows the user to enter data in response to a prompt, including an optional question mark. This is particularly useful for small amounts of input, such as names or dates etc. e.g.

```
100 INPUT "ENTER YOUR NAME ",name$
110 PRINT name$
```

The inclusion of the prompt "ENTER YOUR NAME" is intended to tell the user what is required, and omission of the comma will suppress the question mark when line 100 is executed.

For entering large quantities of DATA, however, INPUT is not really suitable since the DATA will not be recorded when the program is SAVED. With READ and DATA statements, a permanent record of the DATA exists after the program has been SAVED.

INPUT, however, is especially useful for entering large quantities of data which are to be written directly to separate disk or cassette files for permanent storage. This important use of INPUT is discussed in later chapters on DATA files, (as opposed to the PROGRAM files which we are currently considering).

INKEY and INKEY$ provide a similar method of data entry to INPUT, except that a time limitation for the user's response is specified in brackets (in hundredths of a second).

```
10 key=INKEY(100)
20 PRINT key
```

Note that whereas INKEY returns the **ASCII code** for the key pressed, INKEY$ returns the actual character.

GET and GET$

These functions wait until a key is pressed before program execution continues. In BBC BASIC GET actually returns the ASCII code for the key pressed, while GET$ returns the character itself.

```
10 A=GET
20 PRINT A
30 GOTO 10
```

Fig. 2.8 Using GET to print the ASCII code of the key presssed

The above example will print the ASCII code for whatever key is pressed (a full list of these codes appears in the User Guide for the BBC Micro).

So if we run this program and press B, 66 will appear on the screen, i.e. the ASCII code for the letter B.

If we now enter and run the program shown in Fig. 2.9, we find that the actual keyboard characters are displayed, not their ASCII codes as in the previous example.

```
10 A$=GET$
20 PRINT A$
30 GOTO 10
```

Fig. 2.9 Using GET$ to display any key pressed

INPUT and GET, and GET$ are particularly useful in data processing work when it is necessary to give the user a choice of options or respond to a simple question, such as "ENTER Y OR N TO FINISH."

These aspects of the work are covered in greater detail in the chapters on menus and decision making.

Summary

Entering the data may be summarised as follows:
Variable names should convey some idea of the contents of the store e.g. *price, name$*.

When the number of records to be entered in DATA statements is not known, or may be altered, it is better to use REPEAT ... UNTIL, testing for a 'dummy' end of data marker.

```
REPEAT

. . . . . .

. . . . . .

UNTIL name$(I) = "***"
```

Similarly with all-numeric DATA, the dummy may be some ridiculous number like -9999 etc., which would be unlikely to occur as a genuine item of DATA.

If the number of records is known, then a FOR ... NEXT loop is faster, and saves the need for a counter to be incremented e.g. I% = I% + 1. The use of integer variables (I% etc.) saves time and memory space, but does not improve clarity of presentation.

DATA statements are easier to follow if each statement contains one complete record, rather than multiple records.

Lower case letters for variables enhance readability, but are recognised as different from the corresponding upper case version. Hence *WAGE* would be treated as different from *wage*, and allowance will need to be made for this in any alphabetical sorting etc. (to be covered later).

Most data processing programs may be divided into separate blocks or modules, which can be separated by blank lines. It is convenient to place the block of DATA at the end of the program to allow room for expansion at a later date.

Listings are easier to understand if the LISTO7 command is used to provide extra spacing and indent any REPEAT ... UNTIL and FOR ... NEXT loops.

Now that we have discussed the way to enter the DATA into the computer's memory, we will next look at some of the ways of displaying it on the screen.

In the next chapter it is assumed that the reader will have read the appropriate sections of the user guide which describe the various graphics modes. For most data processing work teletext Mode 7 will be adequate, but this does not preclude excursions into other Modes to produce attractive coloured displays for titles, menus or graphical output. The latter is covered later in this book, as a separate appendix.

3

Screen Display

The whole object of data processing is to provide useful output. While this may sometimes be in the form of 'hard copy' i.e. printed on paper, for many applications results displayed on the screen will be adequate. For instance, a quick glance at a VDU would be enough to determine a bank balance, or the owner of a stolen car.

Obviously the information must be displayed clearly and attractively. If any instructions or prompts to the user are necessary they should be clear, friendly and unambiguous. If possible, control of the speed of the display should rest with the user, and the screen should only display the information which is currently necessary. Therefore frequent clearing of the screen should take place to remove 'garbage'.

We will now develop a simple program to read and display a file of cars for sale in a dealer's showroom. We will need string stores for make, model and year of manufacture. Price may be subject to calculation, so this must be stored in a numeric store. Using suitable variable names, there will be no need for REM statements to describe these stores.

A first attempt at this program is shown in Fig. 3.1.

```
10    DIM make$(100),model$(100)
20    DIM year$(100),price(100)
30    I=0
40    REPEAT
50      I=I+1
60      READ make$(I),model$(I),year$(I)
70      READ price(I)
80    UNTIL make$(I)="***"
90
100   FOR N=1 TO I-1
105     CLS
110     PRINT "MAKE:  ";make$(N)
120     PRINT "MODEL: ";model$(N)
130     PRINT "YEAR:  ";year$(N)
140     PRINT "PRICE: £";price(N)
150   NEXT N
160
170   DATA RENAULT,5TL,1981,2500
180   DATA MORRIS,MINOR,1962,1500
190   DATA MG,TF,1952,3500
200   DATA FORD,SIERRA,1983,4900
500   DATA ***,***,***,000
```

Fig. 3.1

User control over the screen display

Obviously so few records are not a viable proposition, but they are sufficient to demonstrate the principles involved. Note that the program will not work unless a **complete** set of 'dummy' data is entered at line 500. The program expects string values for *make$, model$, year$,* and a numeric value for *price*, so suitable 'dummies' must be included for each. The dummy data is included at line 500 to allow the data to expand if necessary.

If you enter this program and RUN, it will work, in a fashion, and the records will be displayed. There are several problems, however, concerned with the screen layout and we will now attempt to polish up the presentation in stages as follows.

1 Clear the screen before printing each record.
2 Slow the display down, under the control of the user.
3 Position the display of the record in the centre of the screen.

Clearing the screen is achieved simply by inserting CLS at line 105. Unfortunately this will cause all but the last record to be wiped off before they have been seen. Clearly some sort of time delay must be included such as

```
145 FOR T=1 TO 5000:NEXT T
```

Altering the value of 5000 will enable the user some control over the time the display is on the screen. Shortly we will consider a method which gives the user *complete* control over the speed at which records are displayed.

Next we will try to improve the screen layout. You will probably have used PRINT TAB(X,Y) to place the cursor X columns from the left and Y rows down from the top of the screen. By modifying the PRINT module in lines 110 and 140 we now have:

```
110 PRINT TAB(12,8);"MAKE: ";make$(N)
120 PRINT TAB(12,10);"MODEL: ";model$(N)
130 PRINT TAB(12,12);"YEAR: ";year$(N)
140 PRINT TAB(12,14);"PRICE: £";price(N)
```

Fig. 3.2 Displaying a record at precise locations on the screen

If you incorporate these changes and run the program you now have a simple program to READ and DISPLAY data. If the program is saved on tape or disk you can also keep the data for future use and **update** it by modifying the appropriate DATA statements. The simple idea of the four fields relating to cars for sale may of course be extended to a parameter list of, say, 6 or more variable names.

User control over the screen display

If you are studying a display of details of a car or house for sale, you would want to move on when *you* were ready, not at a time determined by the programmer.

Using the GET statement, execution of the program need only proceed when a specified key is pressed, usually the space bar. This enables the user to display a file of data in a similar way to the Ceefax and Oracle data bases.

The routine for this is as follows:

```
145 PRINT''''';TAB(6);"PRESS SPACE TO CONTINUE"
147 REPEAT UNTIL GET=32
```

Fig. 3.3 Halting the screen display under the control of the user

20 Screen Display

The four single apostrophes in line 145 enable 4 blank lines to be printed before the printing of the message in the inverted commas "PRESS SPACE ......".

The program is temporarily 'frozen' by line 147:

```
147 REPEAT UNTIL GET=32
```

GET can be interpreted as the ASCII code of the next key to be depressed. The REPEAT ... UNTIL loop will not be satisfied until the key whose code is 32 is depressed. This key is the space bar. So execution of the program will only continue when the space bar is pressed. The "PRESS ANY KEY TO CONTINUE" routine sometimes used is less precise than this, since the program would continue if *any* key were accidentally pressed.

Introducing PROCEDURES

A routine such as PRESS SPACE described above is likely to be needed many times in a large program. To save typing the lines every time we need only type them once, then 'call' the routine whenever we need it.

First we must *define* the PROCEDURE with a suitable name, usually in lower case letters. In this example we will call the procedure 'space' and it is defined as follows:

```
200   DEF PROCspace
210   PRINT''''; TAB(6); "PRESS SPACE";
220   PRINT" TO CONTINUE"
230   REPEAT UNTIL GET=32
240   ENDPROC
```

Fig. 3.4 Defining a PROCEDURE

Note that a procedure is always defined by enclosing in

```
DEF PROC .......



... ............



ENDPROC
```

Once the space bar procedure has been defined, we can call it up and use it whenever we need to, simply by including the statement to PROCspace anywhere in the program.

Now we can insert the definition of the PROCEDURE and call the PROCEDURE from line 160 as follows:

```
10   DIM make$(100),model$(100)
20   DIM year$(100),price(100)
30   I=0
40   REPEAT
50      I=I+1
60      READ make$(I),model$(I),year$(I)
70      READ price(I)
80   UNTIL make$(I)="***"
90
```

```
100    FOR N=1 TO I-1
110      CLS
120      PRINT TAB(12,8);"MAKE:  ";make$(N)
130      PRINT TAB(12,10);"MODEL: ";model$(N)
140      PRINT TAB(12,12);"YEAR:  ";year$(N)
150          PRINT TAB(12,14);"PRICE: £";price(N)
160      PROCspace ─────────────────────────────── calling up
170      NEXT N                                    the procedure
180    END
190
200    DEF PROCspace                         ⎫
210    PRINT'''';TAB(6);"PRESS SPACE";       ⎬ definition
220    PRINT" TO CONTINUE"                   ⎬ of
230    REPEAT UNTIL GET=32                   ⎬ procedure
240    ENDPROC                               ⎭
250
260    DATA RENAULT,5TL,1981,2500
270    DATA MORRIS,MINOR,1962,1500
280    DATA MG,TF,1952,3500
290    DATA FORD,SIERRA,1983,4900
300    DATA ***,***,***,000
```

Fig. 3.5 Defining and calling a PROCEDURE

Note that an END statement has been inserted before the procedures are encountered. This prevents the program execution from entering the PROCEDURE unintentionally, which would produce the error message "NO PROC at line 240".

This simple program doesn't really need this particular procedure, but it has been included as a simple introduction to the subject, to be discussed in detail later in this book. It should be appreciated, however, that PROCEDURES are a fundamental part of structured programming, greatly speeding the execution of programs.

Even the short PROCEDURE, PROCspace would be time-consuming if we wrote it from scratch in future programs. By keeping a copy of this procedure in a handy place, it can simply be 'plugged' into future programs without further programming.

We have used the very simple example of displaying car records to illustrate some aspects of screen presentation. It is suggested that the reader should experiment further with this work to include colour and perhaps double height lettering in titles, as described in the user guide. Where large quantities of text are to be displayed on the screen it is often preferable to use lower case lettering to improve legibility.

So far we have covered the entering of data and displaying records on the screen in a presentable form under the control of the user. Computers are much more versatile than this though, and in the next chapter we will consider the way decisions can be made, and how data can be searched for particular items.

4

Searching

The ability to pass through a very large quantity of data at high speed and find a required record is one of the greatest assets of the computer. Whether it is the details of a person in a staff record, or the antidote for a particular poison, it is the speed of **interrogation** which makes electronic data processing a worthwhile proposition.

At the time of preparing the data for entry it will be necessary to decide on the **criteria** on which the search will be based. The additional searching operation can be an independent module (programmed as a procedure), and this results in the following broad structure for the program.

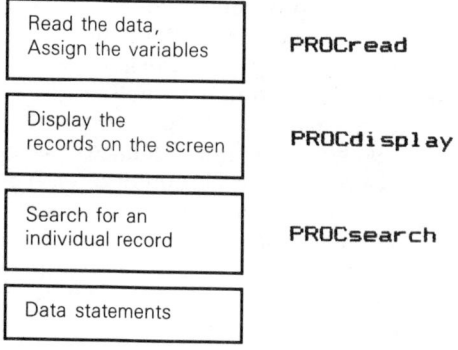

Fig. 4.1 Planning the program as a set of modules

We will again use the car records as a basis for a demonstration program, but it is left as an exercise for the reader to experiment with other types of data, with large and more realistic variable lists.

The program is growing and already the line numbers are inadequate. A modular approach allocating blocks of large line numbers will simplify the problem (Fig. 4.2).

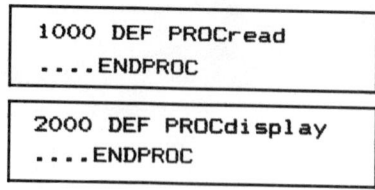

```
3000 DEF PROCsearch
.... ENDPROC
```

```
10000 DATA
.... Statements
```

Fig. 4.2 Allocating blocks of line numbers

These line numbers may seem excessive, but we can use numbers up to 32767 and it will make life easier. Putting the DATA statements at line 10000 ensures that several other modules may later be inserted after the search module.

As an example, let us assume that we wish to search through the records and print all FORD cars. This is no problem, since having assigned all of the records to arrays during the READ module we can pass through the DATA as often as we like, without further READ operations. For example, if the *fourth* car was a FORD,SIERRA,1983, valued at (£)4900, then this data would reside in the subscripted stores as follows:

make$(4) = FORD

model$(4)= SIERRA

year$(4) = 1983

price(4) = 4900

As mentioned earlier, the contents of stores can always be examined after a run of the program by entering, for example:

PRINT year$(4)

On pressing RETURN, 1983 should appear.

Note that the program must be RUN first so that the READ statement can assign the data to the various arrays.

Let us assume then that we have a file of cars and wish to print out all Fords. We set up a FOR ... NEXT loop to pass through all of the cars. Each make of car in the data is compared with the make (FORD) which we provide in an INPUT statement. When a match occurs, the complete record is printed.

A simplified flow chart for this operation is given in Fig. 4.3.

The search module can be coded as follows:

```
3010 INPUT"ENTER THE NAME ",search$
3020 FOR N=1 TO I-1
3030    IF make$(N)=search$ THEN PROCprint
3040    NEXT N
```

Line 3010 enables the user to supply the search name in response to the INPUT prompt, and this is assigned to the store *search$*.

Line 3020 sets up the FOR ... NEXT loop to pass through the data. You may remember that we stop the loop at $N = I - 1$ to prevent printing the end of DATA marker "***" etc.

Line 3030 is the decision line which says:
'If the make of car in the record currently being examined is the same as that input by the user then carry out PROCprint.' (As yet we have not defined PROCprint but its name

24 Searching

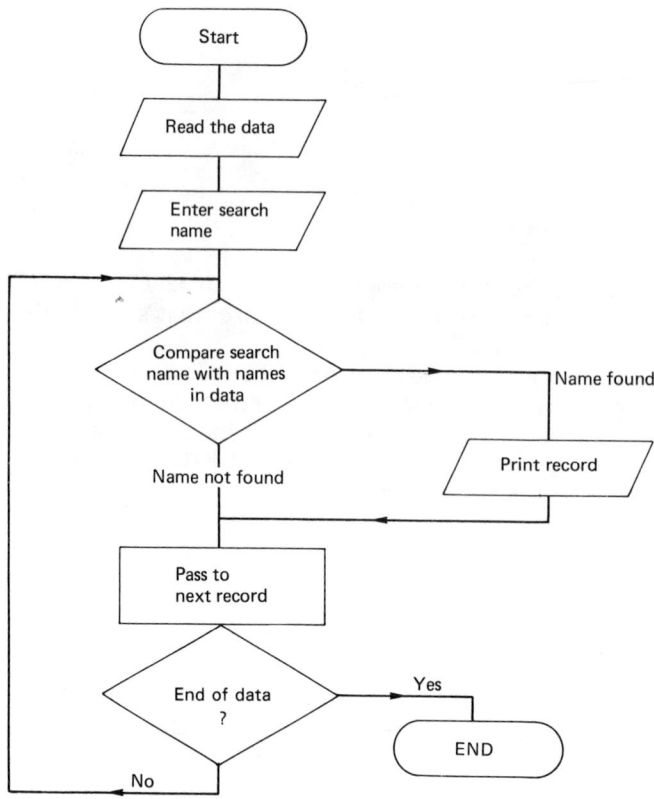

Fig. 4.3

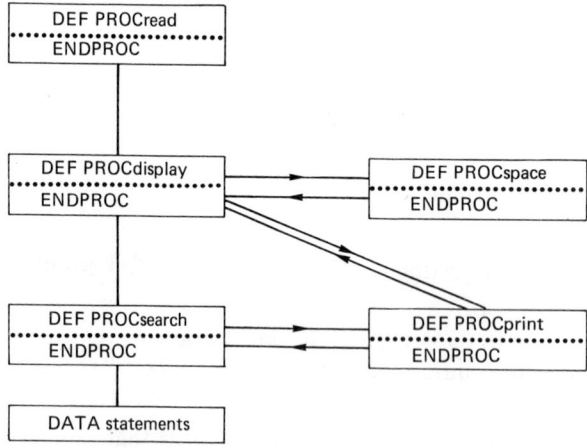

Fig. 4.4 Defining the procedures at the 'end' of the program

```
100   DIM make$(100),model$(100)
110   DIM year$(100),price(100)
120
130   PROCread
140
150   PROCdisplay
160
170   PROCsearch
180
190   END
200
210   DEF PROCread
220    I=0
230    REPEAT
240      I=I+1
250      READ make$(I),model$(I),year$(I)
260      READ price(I)
270      UNTIL make$(I)="***"
280   ENDPROC
290
300   DEF PROCdisplay
310    FOR N=1 TO I-1
320      PROCprint
330      NEXT N
340   ENDPROC
350
360   DEF PROCsearch
370    CLS:PRINT'''''
380    INPUT"ENTER THE NAME "search$
390    FOR N=1 TO I-1
400      IF make$(N)=search$ THEN PROCprint
410      NEXT N
420   ENDPROC
430
440   DEF PROCprint
450    CLS
460    PRINTTAB(12,8);"MAKE:  ";make$(N)
470    PRINTTAB(12,10);"MODEL: ";model$(N)
480    PRINTTAB(12,12);"YEAR:  ";year$(N)
490    PRINTTAB(12,14);"PRICE: £";price(N)
500    PROCspace
510   ENDPROC
520
530   DEF PROCspace
540    PRINT''''';TAB(6);"PRESS SPACE";
550    PRINT" TO CONTINUE"
560    REPEAT UNTIL GET=32
570   ENDPROC
580
590   DATA RENAULT,5TL,1981,2500
600   DATA MORRIS,MINOR,1962,1500
610   DATA MG,TF,1952,3500
620   DATA FORD,SIERRA,1983,4900
630   DATA FORD,GRANADA,1984,8400
640   DATA RENAULT,18GTS,1981,2795
650   DATA VW,SCIROCCO,1979,3295
660   DATA ***,***,***,000
```

Fig. 4.5 A simple program to show the use of procedures

26 Searching

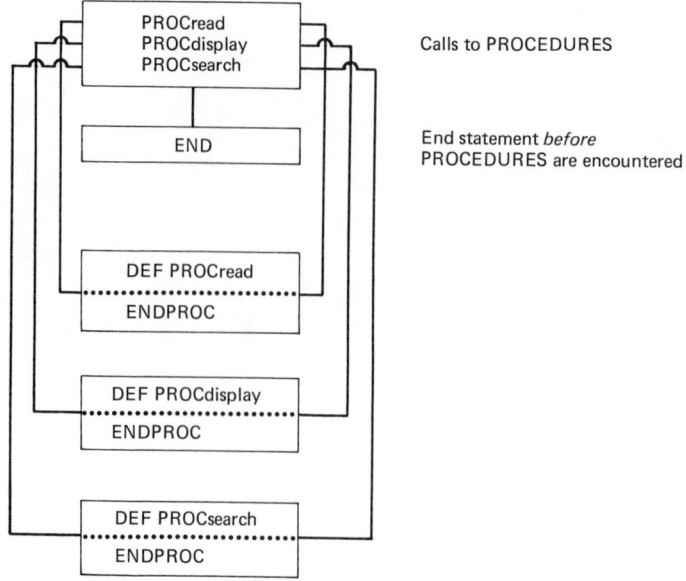

Fig. 4.6 The broad outline of a car program

implies its function. This is one of the advantages of the procedure over its predecessor, the subroutine. The old GOSUB 5000, for example, gave no clue as to what it was doing.)

So if the search name is found in the data the complete record is printed by PROCprint before proceeding to line 3040 and continuing to pass through the data, to search for further records having the search name.

At this stage it is worth pointing out that an alternative search might seek a *unique* name such as a code number, an employee number or a bank account number.

A well-written program will, of course, anticipate the likelihood of the name not being found. It will therefore be necessary to give the user the opportunity to try an alternative spelling. Since lower case letters are regarded as different from upper case, we must also be consistent in the data and the search name, using the same case in both.

We will now rewrite the complete car program, to include the procedures to display, search and print the required records (see Fig. 4.4). The broad outline of the program is shown in Fig. 4.6 and the listing is given in Fig. 4.5.

Note that in Fig. 4.5 the program has a simple overall structure. Apart from the initial dimension statements it is a set of calls to procedures followed by the definitions of these procedures.

It is necessary to include the END statement before the first DEF PROC, since the definitions should not be entered without being called. Note that the procedures PROCspace and PROCprint are called from within other procedures. This is legitimate, although it is a move in the wrong direction if we are aiming for structured programming. Ideally the procedure definition should only have one entrance and one exit, otherwise we start to have the 'sphaghetti' type branching caused by the proliferation of GOTOs in non-structured programming.

Omission of REM statements

No REM statements appear in the program (Fig. 4.5) for the following reasons:

- The choice of meaningful variable names should make the contents of the stores obvious.
- The name used in the PROC and DEF PROC statements should make the purpose of the procedure clear.

Speeding up the program

Integer variables could be used to make the program run faster, but these have been omitted to make the listings easier to read. To obtain this advantage, change all Is to I% and all Ns to N%.

```
240 I%=I%+1
```

Similarly any NEXT statement such as 410 NEXT N is faster if the N is omitted.

```
410 NEXT
```

However, for the sort of work we are discussing and the small quantities of data being processed, the increase in speed resulting from these modifications does not compensate for the loss of clarity in the presentation.

The use of procedures rather than their predecessor, the subroutine, also results in increased speed. In very large programs the time taken to find a subroutine at the end of a program is greater than the time to call a corresponding procedure.

Using the program

The program, as it has developed so far, may be run and will display the catalogue of cars, under the control of the user. After the last car has been displayed the program enables the user to search for a particular make of car, such as FORD. If FORD is entered in response to "ENTER THE NAME" all FORDS in the DATA should be printed on the screen. This is fine if the name entered by the user actually exists in the data. If it doesn't then a message should appear and the user should be instructed to try an alternative spelling.

Of course, if the data is in lower case lettering and we enter a name in upper case, this name will not be found since the two will be regarded as quite different. However, since the upper case alphabet has ASCII codes from 65–90 and the lower case ranges from 97–122, it is possible to test for this and correct if necessary.

Searching for partial names

It is highly likely that the user may not remember the exact spelling of a name. Perhaps a witness to an accident saw only the first few letters of a registration number or we may wish to identify those people whose first name is Jill, say. Alternatively we may have attached codes to the end of names to denote male or female. Using the LEFT$, RIGHT$ and MID$ statements, we can modify our search procedure to identify names which

- **Start** with a certain character or group of characters (LEFT$)
- **Contain** somewhere within them a certain character or group of characters (MID$).
- **Finish** with a certain character or group of characters (RIGHT$).

Searching for names which start with a certain character or group of characters

For simplicity we will base our search on the rather limited data in our previous program (Fig. 4.5). Let us assume that we need to display all cars beginning with the letter M. We would type in M when the screen displays "ENTER THE NAME", and M would be stored in *search$*. We must now compare *search$* with the first letter of all the makes in the data during the FOR ... NEXT loop in PROCsearch.

This is achieved by

```
400 IF LEFT$(make$(N),1)=search$ THEN PROCprint
```

This line can be interpreted as
'If the left-most (1) character in string *make$(N)* is the same as the contents of store *search$* then carry out the print procedure'. In other words all records with names beginning with M will be printed. In this case the MORRIS and MG cars will be displayed.

The use of LEFT$ can be extended to include not just the left-hand letter of a string, but any number of letters, up to the whole string. Supposing a person knew that the name began with the letters REN ... and we wished to find all names in this category. We will now **count** the number of letters (or characters) being searched for and entered into *search$* by the input statement. This is done by the use of LEN(*search$*). If we enter REN in response to "ENTER THE NAME" then LEN(search$) will be LEN("REN"), i.e. 3.

Line 400 now becomes

```
400 IF LEFT$(make$(N),LEN(search$))=search$ THEN PROCprint
```

So we are now entering 3 characters to be searched for on the left of every name in the data. Line 3030 now means 'If the left-most 3 characters of string *make$(N)* are the same as the contents of store *search$* then print the record using PROCprint'.

Note that if we enter 4 characters in *search$* then LEN*(search$)* will equal 4, and so on. This still allows us to enter the complete name if it is known. If we enter RENAULT then LEN(*search$*) = LEN("RENAULT") = 7 and we will look at the 7 left-most characters of *make$(N)*.

The use of RIGHT$ is identical to the use of LEFT$ in every respect except, of course, that we are examining the right-most character or characters.

MID$

This is slightly more complex than LEFT$ and RIGHT$.
Consider the following:

```
20 A$="ELECTRON"

30 PRINT MID$(A$,3,5)
```

Line 30 says 'Print on the screen 5 characters, taken from string A$, starting with the third. When lines 20 and 30 are run ECTRO should be displayed'. Repeat lines 20 and 30 varying the contents of A$ and the numbers X,Y in MID$(A$,X,Y) to obtain a thorough understanding of MID$.

MID$ can therefore be included in the search module to identify these records whose names contain, *anywhere* within them, the required character or group of characters. For instance, if we knew that a registration number contained the letters EA, in this order, all cars containing these letters somewhere within them would be listed.

Checking whether a string contains another string

We will demonstrate this process using a separate independent program. In practice this could be inserted as a module into our search procedure, with suitable modification to the line numbers. We will refer to the letters being searched for as the 'mid-string' and the string being examined as the data string.

Suppose the 'mid-string' were ACT, and we needed to identify all words containing these letters. If we tested, say, the word CHARACTER, we would have to compare ACT, first with CHA, then with HAR, then with ARA, then RAC until a match were found. A short program to demonstrate this is as follows:

```
10   CLS
20   INPUT'' "ENTER THE DATA "data$
30   INPUT'' "MID STRING "m$
40   FOR N=1 TO LEN(data$)
50     IF MID$(data$,N,LEN(m$))=m$ THEN PROCprint
60   NEXT N
70   END
80   DEF PROCprint
90   PRINT'';data$;" contains ";m$
100  ENDPROC
```

Fig. 4.7

This little program itself is of no practical use (since we can see the answer before we run it), but the basic routine could be inserted into the search procedure searching a large amount of data. Note that the 'mid-string' could be a single character or a complete word.

The FOR ... NEXT loop is set up to effect the successive comparisons from left to right along the data string. So with N initially set at 1 we start at the left-hand side of the data string and work across as N is incremented. The terminating value in the loop LEN*(data$)*, means the last character in the data string. In practice if you are searching for more than one character as the mid-string, you will not need to repeat the loop to this last position. However, run this program with various different mid-strings and data strings and you will find it works, including the case when the mid-string is the same as the data string.

This more flexible method of searching has many applications. A register of names could be searched to identify all those people who had the name JOHN at some position in a string containing their complete name. Similarly those people who had included "BADMINTON" in a long string of hobbies could be selected and printed.

```
hobbies$(19)="READING,SWIMMING,BADMINTON,MOTORING"

hobbies$(20)="SNOOKER,GOLF,BRIDGE,RIDING"

hobbies$(21)="SKYDIVING,COOKERY,TENNIS,WALKING"

hobbies$(22)="BADMINTON,CRICKET,GOLF,RACING"
```

The above might be read into array *hobbies$(I)* for a list of employees or students. Note that if commas are used then when this information is entered in DATA statements, the whole string must be enclosed in inverted commas.

Using the previous search routine and entering BADMINTON as the mid-string, M$, we could examine array *hobbies$* by a comparison such as

```
IF MID$(hobbies$(I),N,LEN(M$))=M$ THEN PROCprint
```

Everyone whose list of hobbies included BADMINTON would then have their complete record printed out by a suitable procedure called by PROCprint.

As mentioned earlier we should also provide for the condition where a mid-string is not found and include a suitable message to inform the user that the search was unsuccessful.

Speed

When searching through a large number of records in a practical program it would be possible to speed up the search routine time by

1. Integer rather than floating point variables
   (e.g. I% instead of I)
   N% instead of N).
2. Omitting the variable in the NEXT statement
   (e.g. NEXT instead of NEXT N%)

Searching for records satisfying more than one criterion

We have now considered searching through a list of records to find a particular name or part of a name. This in a data file of cars would, say, yield all FORD or all LEYLAND cars. Such a search on a single field such as the name may not be precise enough and at a particular time it may be necessary to find, say, all FORD ESCORT models.

Returning to our search procedure in Fig. 4.5, we can simply amend the text at line 400 to

```
400 IF make$(N)=search$ AND model$(N)=find$ THEN PROCprint
```

The use of AND means that we only satisfy the IF ... THEN and proceed to PROCprint if the car is *both* FORD *and* ESCORT. We would also need to give the user the opportunity to INPUT the required model with, say,

```
385 INPUT"ENTER THE MODEL"find$
```

and in the example given, store *find$* would contain ESCORT.

This idea could be extended even further to pick out all FORD ESCORTS of a certain year, or colour (if the DATA statements contained it). We simply add another test to line 560 as follows:

```
400 IF make$(N)=search$ AND model$(N)=find$ AND year$(N)=age$
        THEN PROCprint
```

where *make$(N)*, *model$(N)* and *year$(N)* are the make, year and model of the cars supplied in the DATA statements. *search$*, *find$* and *age$* are the make, year and model INPUT by the user in response to INPUT prompts during the running of the program.

A practical program might include a variable list of perhaps 6 or 8 different fields per record and we should now be able to write modules to search for records which satisfy one or more criteria. This searching has been done on the basis of **equality** i.e. in simplified form IF A$ = B$ THEN PROC ....

Searching can also identify those records which contain numerical fields which are greater than (>) or less than (<) a particular numerical value. As a reminder, the full list of BASIC inequality operators is

>   greater than   <   less than
>= greater than or   <= less than or equal to
    or equal to

Using these in our car program, we could for example, print out all cars with a price under £2000.

```
400 IF price(N) < limit THEN PROCprint
```

Again this would be part of the FOR ... NEXT loop which passes through the whole file, comparing *price(N)* of all records in the data array, with *limit*, the price entered by the user. The required price might be input by the user in response to a line such as

```
375 INPUT"ENTER YOUR MAXIMUM PRICE" limit
```

Similarly, to find all cars **above** a certain price then we would replace < with > in line 400.

If we wish to **include** the actual limit then we must use <= or >=.

```
400 IF price(N) <= limit THEN PROCprint
```

The inclusion of = would mean that if a price limit of £2000 were INPUT, then cars at exactly £2000 would be printed as well as those at, say, £1500, £1600, £1900.

Searching for records within a certain numerical range

Now, if purchasing a car, or a house, we will have a **range** of affordable prices i.e. both an upper and a lower limit. A car priced between £3000 and £4000 would be identified by a line such as

```
400 IF price(N) > 3000 AND price(N) < 4000
    THEN PROCprint
```

Note that it is necessary to repeat the name *price(N)* after AND. Also note that in this search we will not find the cars with prices of exactly £3000 and £4000. (Do not include the £ sign in your data—you will then be trying to enter a string into a numeric store). To **include** both £3000 and £4000 we need

```
400 IF price(N) >=3000 AND price(N) <= 4000
    THEN PROCprint
```

During the search module, it is better to program the text as, say,

```
IF...THEN PROCprint
```

rather than IF ... THEN 5000 etc.

This is because the PROCprint, apart from being fast, tells the reader what is happening. IF ... THEN 5000 on the other hand could be the start of a tortuous route through several lines of 'spaghetti'. Wherever possible, the use of IF ... THEN and GOTO to branch to line numbers should be avoided.

Some of the practical applications of these ideas might include the following

Searching

operations:

- Examine a personnel file and print out all employees within a certain salary or age range.
- Check a stock file and print out all items which are below the re-order level.
- Interrogate an estate agent's file and pick out all houses in a particular price range, locality or possessing particular features.
- Display a list of all customers exceeding their credit limit.
- Enter a patient's name and display their medical history.
- Input the part number of a particular component and obtain the operations needed in its manufacture.

Summary

You should now be able to write a program, using procedures to:

1. Read a large number of records.
2. Display each record on the screen.
3. Search for and display any field (string of characters) or part of a field using LEFT$, MID$ and RIGHT$.
4. Identify and display all records containing numerical fields above, below or within a range of numerical values.

Revision of some ideas on structure

Plan the program as a series of modules.
Use meaningful variable names.
Use procedures (rather than subroutines).
Avoid branching whenever possible (avoid GOTOs and IF ... THEN (line number)).

Now that we have covered two important modules (DISPLAY and SEARCH), the next chapter looks at ways of running modules independently.

5

Menus and Procedures

In this chapter we will look at ways of giving the user control over the parts of the program which are executed during a particular run of the program. The simple car program considered so far will work in a fashion.

A typical strategy would be to enter the program and a small amount of data for testing purposes. When the program is 'debugged' i.e. free from errors, it would be advisable to SAVE a copy of the program complete with its limited amount of test DATA. It would then be helpful to prepare the main block of data on paper and check for the following points:

- The DIMension statement contains a number which is greater than or equal to the number of records to be entered in DATA statements.
- The pieces of DATA match exactly the expectations of the READ statement e.g.

    READ A$,B$,C

    expects every record in the DATA to contain two string fields followed by a numeric field.

    A suitable DATA line compatible with this READ statement would be

    1000 DATA ACORN,ELECTRON,32

- The last line of DATA should contain a **complete** dummy record e.g.

    10000 DATA ***,***,0

    for a record containing two strings and one numeric field.

So this program would form a simple file of DATA which could be displayed and searched. Whenever needed the program and its DATA would be LOADed from disk or cassette and RUN. Perfectly useful work can be done using this unsophisticated method. Alterations can be made to DATA statements to update the file containing the latest DATA before the program is saved.

One of the main disadvantages of this program though, is that all of the modules must be executed, even if we only want to search for a name. A real data program might have several modules such as searching, alphabetical sorting, calculating, amending or printing in different formats.

Obviously a set of options is needed so that we run only those parts of the program which are required at a particular time.

34 *Menus and Procedures*

The MENU

Using the limited modules covered so far in this book, we can

```
Read DATA and assign
to arrays
```

```
Display the entire
DATA on the screen
```

```
Search for a name
and print the record
```

Fig. 5.1

We will always need to read the DATA so that this is a compulsory rather than optional module. This simple program, therefore, could have three options.

```
1   Display the entire file
2   Search for a name
3   End
```

Fig. 5.2

Programming the menu can be achieved in a REPEAT ... UNTIL loop as follows:

```
150 REPEAT
160     PROCmenu
170     IF option=1 THEN PROCdisplay
180     IF option=2 THEN PROCsearch
190     UNTIL option=3
200 END
210
220 DEF PROCmenu
230 CLS
240 PRINTTAB(8,8);"1:Display the File"
250 PRINTTAB(8,10);"2:Search for name"
260 PRINTTAB(8,12);"3:End"
270 PRINTTAB(8,16);"Enter your option "
280 PRINTTAB(8,18);"Either 1,2 or 3"
290     option=GET-48
300 ENDPROC
```

Fig. 5.3

This REPEAT ... UNTIL loop becomes the heart of the program. Whichever option you choose is selected by entering 1, 2 or 3 in response to the GET statement at line 290.

The IF ... THEN statements at lines 170 and 180 call up the required PROCEDURES.

After the particular procedure has been executed control of the program is returned to the MENU. This process continues under the control of the user until it is required to end the program by typing 3. This satisfies the terminating condition UNTIL option = 3 in the REPEAT ... UNTIL loop so we exit from the loop. The END statement at line 200 causes this run of the program to cease.

Fig. 5.4 shows a simplified diagram of the program considered as a set of modules.

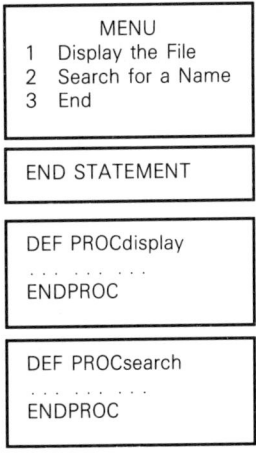

Fig. 5.4 Calling the required Procedure using a Menu

The program is now said to be MENU DRIVEN. The entire running consists of starting from the menu, executing various procedures as required, before returning to the menu to make a further choice.

For simplification some of the minor procedures in the previous program (Fig.4.5), such as PROCprint and PROCspace, have been omitted from Fig.5.4.

In practice you would probably have more options than in the simple menu in Fig.5.4, but if you have too many choices the user may be confused. For example, you may wish to include options to PRINT on the screen, or on paper (or both). In this case, the main menu could direct you to PROCprint, which would contain a further sub-menu giving the secondary options.

Obviously as the menu is going to be the most frequently used part of the program, it should be laid out as clearly and attractively as possible, perhaps using lower case letters, colour, and well-spaced, incorporating PRINT TAB(X,Y).

Entering the option

There are several alternatives for entering the option choice from the menu. We will assume that the user types a choice such as 1, 2 or 3 rather than the initial letter of the option ("Type E to End etc.") The alternatives for entering a number such as 1, 2 or 3 include the following:

INPUT

```
270 INPUT "ENTER YOUR OPTION",option
```
or
```
270 INPUT "ENTER YOUR OPTION" option
```

Omitting the comma, as shown in the second example, suppresses the question mark when the program is run. Both of the above examples will supply the value of *option* directly for use in the next part of PROCmenu, i.e. IF option = 1 THEN PROCdisplay etc. If a

36 Menus and Procedures

letter is accidentally pressed instead of 1, 2 or 3 then *option* takes the value 0, but the program will not crash—it will simply continue until a valid number is entered. A disadvantage with INPUT is that it is necessary to press RETURN, before the program continues. To overcome this, we will consider two more alternatives for entering our options during PROCmenu.

GET and GET$

The format for using these would be as follows:

```
270 PRINT "ENTER YOUR OPTION 1,2 or 3"

280 option = GET
```

The problem with GET is that if either 1, 2 or 3 is entered these actual numbers will not be assigned to the store labelled *option*. Instead *option* will contain either 49, 50 or 51, the ASCII codes for 1, 2 and 3. This will not be compatible with the rest of PROCmenu.

  i.e. `IF option = 1 THEN PROCdisplay`

unless *option* is modified by a line such as

`option = GET-48`

This part of the program would then become

```
280 PRINT"Enter your option 1,2 or 3"

290 option = GET-48
```

The reader not familiar with ASCII codes may well find the above 'fudging' a bit confusing, so a fourth alternative for entering the option is shown below:

```
280 PRINT"Enter your option 1,2 or 3"

290 option$=GET$
```

As with the previous example using GET, the program will accept a number (or letter) without any apparent problem. The problem now is that if, say, we enter 3 to end the program, *option$* will contain not the mathematical number 3 but the character 3. (The reader unfamiliar with this idea should think of the digits in a telephone number. They have no mathematical place value like hundreds, tens and units). Similarly when numbers are assigned to string stores like *option$* they have no mathematical meaning. However, the string contents of store GET$ can be easily converted to the numeric contents of store *option* by the use of the value function VAL.

  Our two line routine for entering the options then becomes

```
220 PRINT"Enter your option 1,2 or 3"

230 option = VAL(GET$)
```

Of the four alternatives discussed, the two INPUT methods are probably the least confusing, while GET and GET$ are faster.

  This menu can be inserted into our main program and it enables the user to select which procedures to run at a particular time. No matter what key is pressed, there are only four possible outcomes.

Entering the option 37

1 Execute a procedure and return to the menu.
2 Accidentally press a wrong key, but still remain within the menu until a correct option is selected.
3 Enter 3 and leave the program.
4 Leave the program using ESCAPE or BREAK.

A further modification would be to program the computer to return to the MENU if an error occurs. This can be done using

```
ON ERROR GOTO ...
```

After GOTO we insert the line number for the start of the MENU, so in this case we could use

```
100 ON ERROR GOTO 150
```

The ESCAPE key is also classified as an ERROR so with a line such as line 100 included, pressing ESCAPE will now return us to the MENU. Now we can only exit from the program using the deliberate option (3 in this case) or by pressing BREAK.

During the process of developing a program there will inevitably be errors and unfortunately ON ERROR GOTO will mask them by suppressing the error message. It is therefore advisable not to include ON ERROR GOTO ... until the program has been fully tested and debugged.

We can now convert the previous car program, Fig. 4.5, into its menu-driven form. It is simply a case of slotting the menu into the beginning of the program. The complete program is shown in Fig. 5.5. Note that after the program has been debugged it has been RENUMBERED in steps of 10.

To make the listing easier to read, the following have been used:

- Lower case letters for variable names and names of PROCEDURES
- In general, single statement lines.
- Blank lines to separate modules.
- LISTO7 to improve spacing and highlights the REPEAT ... UNTIL loops.

```
100  DIM make$(100),model$(100)
110  DIM year$(100),price(100)
120
130  PROCread
140
150  REPEAT
160     PROCmenu
170     IF option=1 THEN PROCdisplay
180     IF option=2 THEN PROCsearch
190  UNTIL option=3
200  END
210
220  DEF PROCmenu
230  CLS
240  PRINTTAB(8,8);"1:Display the File"
250  PRINTTAB(8,10);"2:Search for name"
260  PRINTTAB(8,12);"3:End"
270  PRINTTAB(8,16);"Enter your option "
280  PRINTTAB(8,18);"Either 1,2 or 3"
290  option=GET-48
300  ENDPROC
310
```

38 Menus and Procedures

```
320   DEF PROCread
330   I=0
340   REPEAT
350     I=I+1
360     READ make$(I),model$(I),year$(I)
370     READ price(I)
380   UNTIL make$(I)="***"
390   ENDPROC
400
410 DEF PROCdisplay
420 FOR N=1 TO I-1
440   PROCprint
490   NEXT N
500 ENDPROC
510
520   DEF PROCsearch
530   CLS:PRINT'''''
540 INPUT"ENTER THE NAME "search$
550 FOR N=1 TO I-1
560   IF make$(N)=search$ THEN PROCprint
570   NEXT N
580 ENDPROC
590
600   DEF PROCprint
610 CLS
620 PRINTTAB(12,8);"MAKE:  ";make$(N)
630 PRINTTAB(12,10);"MODEL: ";model$(N)
640 PRINTTAB(12,12);"YEAR:  ";year$(N)
650 PRINTTAB(12,14);"PRICE: £";price(N)
660 PROCspace
670   ENDPROC
680
690   DEF PROCspace
700   PRINT'''''';TAB(6);"PRESS SPACE";
710   PRINT" TO CONTINUE"
720   REPEAT UNTIL GET=32
730   ENDPROC
740
750 DATA RENAULT,5TL,1981,2500
760 DATA MORRIS,MINOR,1962,1500
770 DATA MG,TF,1952,3500
780 DATA FORD,SIERRA,1983,4900
790 DATA FORD,GRANADA,1984,8400
800 DATA RENAULT,18GTS,1981,2795
810 DATA VW,SCIROCCO,1979,3295
820 DATA ***,***,***,000
```

Fig. 5.5 A menu-driven program to search for and display car records

Obviously the amount of DATA shown in Fig.5.5 is totally inadequate for a viable computer program. The program is just intended to show, as simply as possible, the method of running the program as a set of procedures accessed from a menu. PROCread is placed before the menu, since it must be carried out before any of the optional procedures can be carried out.

Using this program as a skeleton, more complex programs may now be developed. We may wish to add further modules, such as for calculation, alphabetical or numerical sorting or printing **hard copy** (diverting output to the paper in a line printer). You could, of course, use this program as it stands to keep simple records. Replace the variable names *make$*, *model$*, *year$* and *price* throughout the program and then add suitable DATA from line 750 onwards. It is essential to include a complete 'dummy' record as the last line of the DATA.

Extending the program

The basic idea of a menu-driven program has been demonstrated using the procedures to display and search records. These are by no means the only operations which our powerful microcomputer can perform on a file of data. It is, however, a very simple matter now to extend the program to include any further operations by simply programming them as procedures. Typical additional procedures might be to sort into alphabetical order or to do some calculation. Whatever the purpose of the extra procedures, the general method for incorporating them into an existing program (Fig.5.5) would be:

1 Extend the menu.
2 Program the call to the new procedure(s).
3 DEFine the new PROCedure(s).

This general method will apply whatever the program or the nature of the DATA being processed. For simplicity we will continue with the car records used previously (Fig.5.5) and incorporate a procedure to **calculate** new prices based on a % increase. We must, therefore, add a procedure to take the existing prices as input from the data and apply a scale factor. For example, a 10% increase implies a scale factor of

$1 + \frac{10}{100} = 1.10$. The scale factor is therefore $\left(1 + \frac{\text{percentage increase}}{100}\right)$.

This would be programmed in BASIC as

```
price(N) = price(N)*(1+percent/100)
```

In order to apply this scale factor to every record in the DATA we now set up a pass through every record using a FOR ... NEXT loop. FOR ... NEXT is used because we know the number of records—they were previously counted during the READ operation. The number of records is I − 1. (It is necessary to subtract 1, since the stores with subscript I contain the dummy data *** etc.)

To give the user the flexibility to INPUT any percentage increase, this is entered by the statement INPUT percent.

The new calculation module to be inserted is shown in Fig. 5.6.

```
720   DEF PROCpercent
730   CLS
740   PRINT TAB(6,10);"Enter % increase"
750   INPUT percent
760   FOR N=1 TO I-1
770     price(N)=price(N)*(1+percent/100)
780   NEXT N
790   ENDPROC
```

Fig. 5.6

Notice that there is no need to READ the data again. Having read the data originally and assigned it to the arrays *name$(N)*, *model$(N)* etc. it is simply a case of passing through it in a FOR ... NEXT loop.

40 *Menus and Procedures*

This procedure can now be inserted at the end of the program (but before the DATA statements). We must also alter the menu to give this additional option and the complete program is shown in Fig. 5.7.

```
100   DIM make$(100),model$(100)
110   DIM year$(100),price(100)
120
130   PROCread
140
150   REPEAT
160      PROCmenu
170      IF option=1 THEN PROCdisplay
180      IF option=2 THEN PROCsearch
190      IF option=3 THEN PROCpercent
200      UNTIL option=4
210   END
220
230 DEF PROCmenu
240 CLS
250 PRINTTAB(8,8);"1:Display the File"
260 PRINTTAB(8,10);"2:Search for name"
270 PRINTTAB(8,12);"3:Increase prices"
280 PRINTTAB(8,14);"4:End"
290 PRINTTAB(8,18);"Enter your option "
300 PRINTTAB(8,20);"Either 1,2,3 or 4"
310    option=GET-48
320 ENDPROC
330
340   DEF PROCread
350   I=0
360   REPEAT
370      I=I+1
380      READ make$(I),model$(I),year$(I)
390      READ price(I)
400      UNTIL make$(I)="***"
410   ENDPROC
420
430 DEF PROCdisplay
440 FOR N=1 TO I-1
450    PROCprint
460    NEXT N
470 ENDPROC
480
490   DEF PROCsearch
500   CLS:PRINT'''''
510 INPUT"ENTER THE NAME "search$
520 FOR N=1 TO I-1
530    IF make$(N)=search$ THEN PROCprint
540    NEXT N
550 ENDPROC
560
570   DEF PROCprint
580 CLS
590 PRINTTAB(12,8);"MAKE:  ";make$(N)
600 PRINTTAB(12,10);"MODEL: ";model$(N)
610 PRINTTAB(12,12);"YEAR:  ";year$(N)
620 PRINTTAB(12,14);"PRICE: £";price(N)
```

Global and local variables

```
630 PROCspace
640   ENDPROC
650
660   DEF PROCspace
670   PRINT'''''';TAB(6);"PRESS SPACE";
680   PRINT" TO CONTINUE"
690   REPEAT UNTIL GET=32
700   ENDPROC
710
720   DEF PROCpercent
730   CLS
740   PRINT TAB(6,10);"Enter % increase"
750   INPUT percent
760   FOR N=1 TO I-1
770     price(N)=price(N)*(1+percent/100)
780     NEXT N
790   ENDPROC
800
810 DATA RENAULT,5TL,1981,2500
820 DATA MORRIS,MINOR,1962,1500
830 DATA FORD,SIERRA,1983,4900
840 DATA FORD,GRANADA,1984,8400
850 DATA RENAULT,18GTS,1981,2795
860 DATA VW,SCIROCCO,1979,3295
870 DATA ***,***,***,000
```

Fig. 5.7 Inserting an additional procedure (PROCpercent)

If the DATA is extended to provide a realistic file of, say, 200 records, it will be found that the modified prices may be obtained and displayed extremely rapidly. Using a program of this type, perhaps with a different variable list, VAT, etc. could be calculated and displayed in a separate calculating procedure.

Note that after running PROCpercent, as it has been called, the user is returned to the menu without the new prices being displayed. The user should now choose option 1 to display the file, after which each car and its increased price will be displayed. These new prices will only exist in the arrays stored in the memory. The original prices will still be stored on tape or diskette in the DATA statements and cannot be modified without retyping and resaving. Later we will see how DATA FILES may be updated using more sophisticated methods.

Line numbers

As stated earlier, it is helpful in developing a large program to allocate blocks of, say, 1000 to each procedure, to allow room for additional lines to be inserted. Placing the data at the end of the program allows new records to be added without upsetting any of the procedures.

When the program has been tested and the procedures are finalised then it may be appropriate to RENUMBER to give a more reasonable and economical set of line numbers.

Global and local variables

In Fig. 5.7, the variables used have the same value throughout the program. For instance, I is the counter which contains the number of records read during PROCread. After

42 *Menus and Procedures*

PROCread has been executed, this value of I is used in PROCdisplay to display the whole file of records using the statement FOR N = 1 to I − 1.

Similarly, if we run the program (Fig. 5.7) after typing 4 to END, we can examine the state of the variables by using immediate mode.

e.g. PRINT I

PRINT N

With the DATA given in Fig. 5.7 it will be found that I has the value 7 (since record 7 is the dummy data). Similarly N will also contain the value 7, provided in our running of the program we have run either PROCdisplay, PROCsearch or PROCpercent. (Although the FOR ... NEXT loops say FOR N = 1 to I − 1, N actually finishes the loop with the same value as I.)

The behaviour of these variable stores can therefore be summarised as follows:

- Values may be assigned to them in one part of the program, such as assigning 7 to store N in DEF PROCdisplay.
- These values remain throughout subsequent running of the program unless altered by further assignment statements. The value of N assigned in DEF PROCdisplay would hold in any other PROCEDURE. This can be tested as follows:

1 Type RUN and press RETURN.
2 Choose option 1 to display the file.
3 Choose option 4 to End.
4 Type in immediate mode PROCprint and press RETURN.

You should find that the dummy record is displayed. This demonstrates that the value of N assigned during PROCdisplay is carried through and used in PROCprint.

Since the variables such as N and I maintain their latest assigned values throughout the whole program, they are known as **global variables**.

Local variables

It may be desirable to prevent the new value assigned to a variable in one procedure from influencing the value of the same variable used in other procedures. Variables may be **isolated** from their namesake in other parts of the program by declaring them as **local**, e.g. LOCAL N or LOCAL N,I.

This may be demonstrated by the following method, using the program in Fig. 5.7.

1 Declare the variable N to have a local value in PROCdisplay by adding the statement:

    435 LOCAL N

2 Check the local value of N just before leaving DEF PROCdisplay by adding the statement:

    465 CLS:PRINT"LOCAL N"N:PROCspace

3 Check the global value of N after leaving DEF PROCdisplay (but before running any other PROCedures which would assign new values to N). This can be done on exit from the program by the line:

    205 CLS:PRINT"GLOBAL"N:PROCspace

If we enter the above lines, RUN the program, display the file, then End, we should see:

    LOCAL N 7

and GLOBAL N 0

where 7 is the LOCAL value for N at the end of PROCdisplay and N is the GLOBAL value for N existing *before* and *after* the execution of DEF PROCdisplay.

Of course, the choice of N as a local variable was purely for demonstration purposes—it is not necessary in this particular program.

Similar tests will show that by declaring a variable, such as I, as local, its value prior to entry to the procedure is not carried *into* the procedure.

Global and local variables can be summarized as follows:

- Variables will normally have a global value which remains constant throughout the various parts of a program, unless new values are assigned by a LET statement e.g. LET I = I + 1(more simply I = I + 1), or by a FOR ... NEXT loop.
- The value of a variable within a PROCEDURE may be isolated from its values in other parts of the program by declaring it as LOCAL to that PROCEDURE. No values for that variable enter or leave the PROCEDURE in which it is declared local.
- Whenever there is a danger that changes to a variable's contents within a procedure will interfere with the use of the same variable outside the procedure then it should be declared as local.

Summary

At this stage we should be able to write a menu-driven program to store, on tape or disk, a large number of records as DATA statements. Using a menu, we can process the data by displaying the whole file or search and display selected records according to or fulfilling certain criteria. We should also now be able to include a further option to perform calculations on DATA stored in numeric variables. The next section looks at a further option widely used in data processing—the sorting of records into alphabetical or numerical order.

6

Sorting Data

Sorting is the process by which words or numbers are placed in a particular **order**. A typical data handling operation would be to produce a printed list on paper containing the details of all of the personnel in a company. The list would be far easier to scan if the names are in alphabetical order. Similarly, it may be useful to arrange a set of students' names in an order depending on the marks obtained in an examination. Whether the sort is based on arranging words in alphabetical order or arranging numbers in rank order the basic method is the same.

If we realise during the planning of a program that a sort process will be needed then this may affect the format of the data statements. For instance, if the program will need to sort names into alphabetical order, then it would be helpful to place the surname as the first field in the data. We must also remember that lower case letters are treated differently from upper case.

The basic method is to compare the names to be sorted, a pair at a time. This can be achieved by a pass through the data in a FOR ... NEXT loop. The comparison can be made using the inequality sign >, which means 'alphabetically after' when used with names and 'greater than' when used numerically.

At the start of the pass through the data, the first two names are compared. If the names are already in alphabetical order the pass through the loop continues and names 2 and 3 are then compared. If the first two names were not in order they are swapped, i.e. the contents of the subscripted variable stores are exchanged. Part of this process is shown in diagram form in Fig. 6.1.

Swapping the contents of two stores requires three statements. If we find that the contents of *name$(I)* must be exchanged for the contents of *name$(I + 1)* we cannot simply say

```
500 LET name$(I)=name$(I+1)
510 LET name$(I+1)=name$(I)
```

Supposing *name$(I)* originally contained SMITH and *name$(I + 1)* contained JONES. Line 500 would certainly put JONES into store *name$(I)* by overwriting the original contents. However, *name$(I + 1)* will still contain JONES also, since its contents have simply been copied into store *name$(I)*. Line 510 would therefore achieve nothing, since both stores would contain JONES. The problem is that the original contents of *name$(I)* are lost when it is overwritten in line 500. To overcome this we preserve the original contents of store *name$(I)* by temporarily assigning the contents to a holding store, for subsequent recall.

Sorting Data

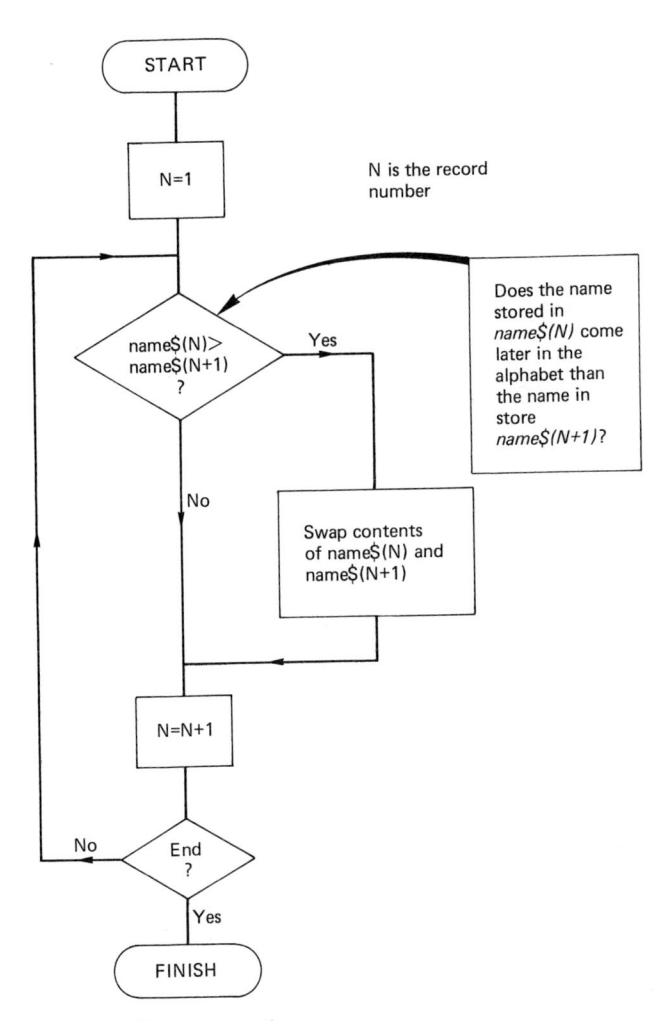

Fig. 6.1 The swap routine

```
500 LET keep$=name$(I)
510 LET name$(I)=name$(I+1)
520 LET name$(I+1)=keep$
```

Fig. 6.2 The swap routine. *keep$* preserves a copy of *name$(I)* before it is overwritten

Line 500 means 'Let store *keep$* contain a copy of the contents of store *name$(I)*.

Line 510 says 'Let store *name$(I)* contain a copy of the contents of store *name$(I + 1)*',

and finally Line 520 says 'Let store *name$(I + 1)* contain a copy of the store *keep$*, which contains the original contents of store *name$(I)*'.

After these three lines, the contents of stores *name$(I)* and *name$(I + 1)* will have been interchanged.

We will develop as a demonstration a small program to sort 6 names into alphabetical

46 Sorting Data

order—again an unrealistically low number compared with practical sorts of hundreds or thousands of names.

It will be necessary to enclose the swap routine in a FOR ... NEXT loop to effect the pass through the data.

```
400 DEF PROCswap
410 LET keep$=name$(I)
420 LET name$(I)=name$(I+1)
430 LET name$(I+1)=keep$
440 ENDPROC
```

Fig. 6.3 Part of a program to sort 6 names into alphabetical order

At the start of the sort process, subscript I will have the value 1, so we start by comparing the contents of store *name$(1)* with *name$(2)*. Finally when I = 5 we compare *name$(5)* with *name$(6)*. In Fig. 6.3 if the two names were not in order, they are exchanged using PROCswap, otherwise the pass through the data continues with no swap taking place.

The program continues through the data until consecutive pieces of data have been sorted in pairs. At this stage, however, the whole list is not yet in alphabetical order and we will illustrate this with six names as follows:

SMITH	BROWN	BROWN	BROWN	BROWN
BROWN	SMITH	JONES	JONES	JONES
JONES	JONES	SMITH	SMITH	SMITH
WALKER	WALKER	WALKER	WALKER	ABLE
ABLE	ABLE	ABLE	ABLE	WALKER
BONNER	BONNER	BONNER	BONNER	BONNER

compared ▢

compared and swapped ▢

Number of swaps = 4

It can be seen from the example that although we have made some progress, the list is still not in alphabetical order, so the process is repeated by passing through the FOR ... NEXT loop again.

BROWN	BROWN	BROWN	BROWN	BROWN
JONES	JONES	JONES	JONES	JONES
SMITH	SMITH	SMITH	ABLE	ABLE
ABLE	ABLE	ABLE	SMITH	BONNER
BONNER	BONNER	BONNER	BONNER	SMITH
WALKER	WALKER	WALKER	WALKER	WALKER

Number of swaps = 2

During the subsequent passes, the words are 'bubbled' up into the correct position, so that this is known as a **bubble sort**.

Sorting Data

Although the names are still not in alphabetical order, we are getting nearer. Eventually a pass through the data will result in no swaps taking place, and the list will then be in alphabetical order. We can easily test for this situation by setting a counter in store *swaps* to zero and incrementing by 1 every time a swap takes place (see Fig. 6.4). If, at the end of the pass, *swaps* = zero, no swaps have taken place, so the list must be in alphabetical order.

In our swap routine, *swaps* must be set to zero **before** we enter the loop, and increased by 1 after each swap has taken place. *swaps* therefore registers the number of swaps on a particular **pass** through all of the data.

```
300 DEF PROCsort
310 C=I-1
320 REPEAT
330    swaps=0
340    FOR I=1 TO C-1
350       IF name$(I)>name$(I+1) THEN PROCswap
360    NEXT I
370    UNTIL swaps=0
380 ENDPROC
390
400 DEF PROCswap
410 keep$=name$(I)
420 name$(I)=name$(I+1)
430 name$(I+1)=keep$
440 swaps=swaps+1
450 ENDPROC
```

Fig. 6.4

At line 370 we test to see if any swaps have been made during the pass through the data, i.e. if *swaps* is equal to 0. If swaps have been made we must return to line 320 and re-pass until no swaps are made, i.e. the list is in alphabetical order.

We will now consider the remainder of the sorting process for the six names. Three more passes will be required before the data is known to be in alphabetical order.

3rd Pass

	BROWN	BROWN	BROWN	BROWN	BROWN
	JONES	JONES	ABLE	ABLE	ABLE
	ABLE	ABLE	JONES	BONNER	BONNER
	BONNER	BONNER	BONNER	JONES	JONES
	SMITH	SMITH	SMITH	SMITH	SMITH
	WALKER	WALKER	WALKER	WALKER	WALKER

Number of swaps = 2

4th Pass

	BROWN	ABLE	ABLE	ABLE	ABLE
	ABLE	BROWN	BONNER	BONNER	BONNER
	BONNER	BONNER	BROWN	BROWN	BROWN
	JONES	JONES	JONES	JONES	JONES
	SMITH	SMITH	SMITH	SMITH	SMITH
	WALKER	WALKER	WALKER	WALKER	WALKER

Number of swaps = 2

48 Sorting Data

After the fourth pass, the names are in alphabetical order, the computer will pass through them again and on counting no swaps (i.e. *swaps* = 0) will leave the sort routine to print the final sorted list.

We have now rearranged the data so that, although the content of the data is unchanged, some or all of it may have been swapped into new stores with different subscripts. In our example, *name$(5)* originally stored ABLE but this was 'bubbled' up in the sorting process until it finally resided in store *name$(1)*.

Now that the data is stored in alphabetical order, it is simply a matter of printing out the sorted list in a FOR ... NEXT loop (Fig. 6.5).

```
470 DEF PROCdisplay
480 FOR I=1 TO C
490    PRINT name$(I)
500    NEXT I
510 ENDPROC
```
Fig. 6.5

We can now put the sort routine into a program to READ a set of names into an array *name$(I)* and sort them into alphabetical order. Finally the sorted list will be displayed.

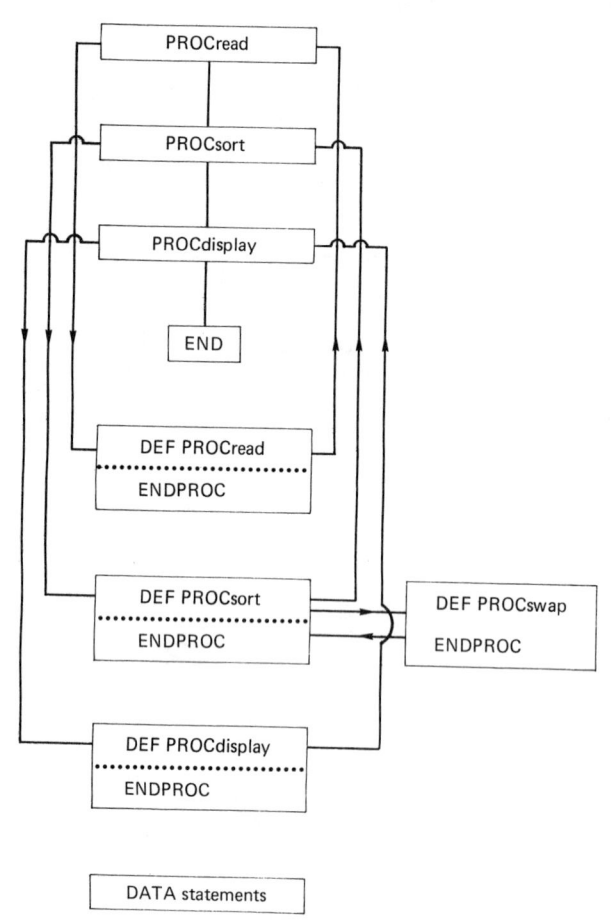

Fig. 6.6 The plan for a program to sort and display a file of names

Sorting Data 49

As all three of these operations (READ, SORT, DISPLAY) are compulsory, there is no need for a menu. The plan for the program is shown in Fig. 6.6.

The complete program to sort a set of names into alphabetical order is shown in Fig. 6.7. It observes the rules mentioned earlier in this book, such as the placing of the procedure definitions after the END statement. The DATA is read until the last record (containing the dummy data "***") is detected. As this dummy record will go into the last array store *name$(I)*, we set the number of records to $C = I - 1$. For these simple one word records I have used many fields per line, in breach of the previous notes on clear, well-spaced DATA.

```
100 DIM name$(110)
110   TIME=0
120
130 PROCread
140
150 PROCsort
160
170 PROCdisplay
180
190   PRINT "TIME "TIME/100" SECS"
200 END
210
220 DEF PROCread
230 I=0
240 REPEAT
250    I=I+1
260    READ name$(I)
270    UNTIL name$(I)="***"
280 ENDPROC
290
300 DEF PROCsort
310 C=I-1
320 REPEAT
330    swaps=0
340    FOR I=1 TO C-1
350       IF name$(I)>name$(I+1)THEN PROCswap
360       NEXT I
370    UNTIL swaps=0
380 ENDPROC
390
400 DEF PROCswap
410 keep$=name$(I)
420 name$(I)=name$(I+1)
430 name$(I+1)=keep$
440 swaps=swaps+1
450 ENDPROC
460
470 DEF PROCdisplay
480 FOR I=1 TO C
490    PRINT name$(I)
500    NEXT I
510 ENDPROC
520
530 DATA MIKE,ANN,JOHN,WILF,CHRIS,TOM
1000 DATA ***
```

Fig. 6.7 A Program to sort names into alphabetical order

50 Sorting Data

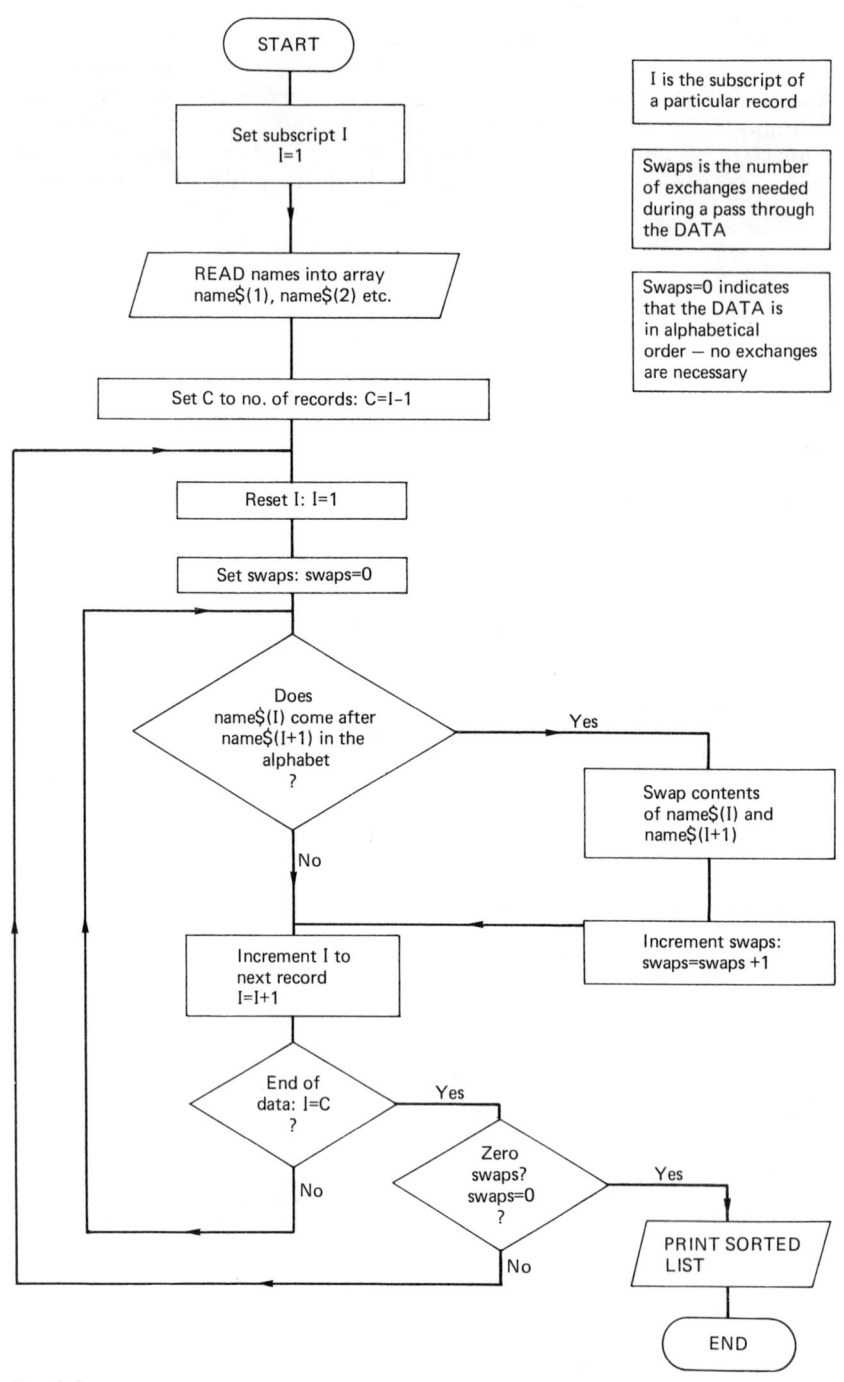

Fig. 6.8

You can use this program for as many names as you like, with the following provisos:

- The number in the dimension statement is greater than or equal to the number of records in the DATA.
- The very last record is the end of DATA dummy "***".

The reader will also notice the use of TIME at lines 110 and 190 and the purpose of this will be explained later.

At this stage it is appropriate to try to appreciate the overall sequence of operations and this is given in the flowchart Fig. 6.8. (Of course, a flowchart, if used at all, should really be drawn *before* the program is written—although in practice this may not always be the case. In fact, flowcharts are becoming somewhat outdated. In this rather complicated routine it is intended to make the process easier to follow.)

When you run a sort program for the first time, you could be forgiven for thinking something was wrong. Instead of the usual lightning response, the screen will display nothing except the flashing cursor. With hundreds of names to sort, this could take a considerable time and it is worth including a message to the user, such as

"Sorting in progress" or similar.

Speeding up the sort process—integer variables

Sorting is a relatively slow process and the 'bubble sort' described in this chapter is not the fastest by any means. However, it can be speeded up. One way to do this is to replace all of the numeric variable stores (C and I) by integer variables (C% and I%). The latter are faster since they are stored as whole numbers, rather than being converted to the more complicated floating point numbers involving bicimals (powers of 2 to a large number of 'bicimal' places).

The complete program, rewritten with integer variables is shown in Fig. 6.9.

The reader may care to enter the first version of the program (Fig. 6.7) and enter a 100 names to be sorted. When the program is RUN, the cursor will flash while the sort proceeds. After a short time, the sorted list will be displayed, followed by the message

TIME XX.XX SECS

The timing of the sort is achieved by the TIME statements at lines 110 and 190.

Now convert all Cs to C% and Is to I% as shown in Fig. 6.9. Rerun the program with the same set of DATA and note the results. When I carried out the test with 100 names, the results obtained were as follows:

Features	Time to sort and display 100 names
Floating point variable names(C,I)	56.77 seconds
Integer variable names(C%,I%)	34.82 seconds

Obviously these are only relative figures, rather than absolute, since the time taken will also depend on the state of the original data i.e. the distance of words from their final destination in the sorted list. It is clear, however, that the integer variables produce a worthwhile saving in time.

52 Sorting Data

```
100 DIM name$(110)
110   TIME=0
120
130 PROCread
140
150 PROCsort
160
170 PROCdisplay
180
190  PRINT "TIME "TIME/100" SECS"
200 END
210
220 DEF PROCread
230 I%=0
240 REPEAT
250     I%=I%+1
260     READ name$(I%)
270     UNTIL name$(I%)="***"
280 ENDPROC
290
300 DEF PROCsort
310 C%=I%-1
320 REPEAT
330    swaps%=0
340    FOR I%=1 TO C%-1
350      IF name$(I%)>name$(I%+1)THEN PROCswap
360      NEXT I%
370    UNTIL swaps%=0
380 ENDPROC
390
400 DEF PROCswap
410 keep$=name$(I%)
420 name$(I%)=name$(I%+1)
430 name$(I%+1)=keep$
440 swaps%=swaps%+1
450 ENDPROC
460
470 DEF PROCdisplay
480 FOR I%=1 TO C%
490    PRINT name$(I%)
500    NEXT I%
510 ENDPROC
520
530 DATA MIKE,ANN,JOHN,WILF,CHRIS,TOM
1000 DATA ***
```

Fig. 6.9 The alphabetic sort program rewritten with integer variables. Note that more DATA must be added, finishing with the dummy ∗∗∗

Ever-decreasing looping

A further increase in speed for the bubble sort can be achieved by studying the process more closely. If we look at the original example of six names, we see that the result of the first pass is to 'dump' the last word, alphabetically, to the end of the list. In other words, at the start of the second pass WALKER is already in its final resting place and need take no further part in the proceedings. Similarly on entry to the third pass SMITH is correctly sorted and so need not be considered further.

This process of pushing the alphabetically latest words to the end of the list means that only the first pass need work through the whole set of data. After the first pass through the complete set of C% records, the next pass need only consider C% − 1 records and so on. This can be achieved by **decrementing** (reducing by 1) C% using a line such as C% = C% − 1.

(Reminder
C% is the total number of records.
To pass through C% records comparing *name$(I)* with *name$(I + 1)*, the FOR ... NEXT loop specifies FOR I = 1 TO C%-1, so that ultimately *name$(C%-1)* is compared with *name$(C%)*.

So now we have to alter PROCsort to pass through the DATA in ever-decreasing loops. This can be achieved by inserting C% = C%−1 at line 365. This will indeed make successive passes compare fewer and fewer records, ignoring the correctly sorted records in their final positions at the end of the list.

Unfortunately, though, because we are changing the value of C% within DEF PROCsort, this will affect the value of C% used elsewhere later in the program. This is precisely the case for LOCAL variables, as previously discussed. The new values generated for C% and I% during DEF PROCsort will no longer be suitable for DEF PROCdisplay, which requires a pass through the **entire** data. Fortunately BBC BASIC has a method of passing values into a procedure, so that any changed value resulting from the action of the procedure does not affect the later use of this variable.

Parameter passing

Referring to Fig. 6.9, we will set C% to contain the total number of records (excluding the 'dummy') by inserting

    275 C% = I%-1

Remember that at the end of the READ operation, I% would be 101 for 100 genuine records plus one 'dummy'.

Now whatever procedure we want to pass this parameter C% to, we include the variable name in both the PROCcall and the DEF PROC as follows:

        150 PROCsort(C%)

        300 DEF PROCsort(C%)

and

        170 PROCdisplay(C%)

        470 DEF PROCdisplay(C%)

Let us summarise this rather complicated operation:

1 Decrementing C% during PROCsort would cause an incorrect value of C% to be passed to PROCdisplay.
2 Setting C% after reading and 'parameter passing' it to PROCsort and PROCdisplay declares C% as a local variable, so that no changed values of C% are transferred out of the procedures.

54 Sorting Data

(It is not necessary when parameter passing to declare variables using the LOCAL statement, as this is implicit in the method.)

Modification of Fig. 6.9 to include the lines 150, 170, 275, 300 and 470 previously described gives the program shown in Fig. 6.10 and the time to sort 100 names is reduced to 26.52 seconds.

```
100 DIM name$(110)
110   TIME=0
120
130 PROCread
140
150 PROCsort(C%)
160
170 PROCdisplay(C%)
180
190   PRINT "TIME "TIME/100" SECS"
200 END
210
220 DEF PROCread
230 I%=0
240 REPEAT
250     I%=I%+1
260     READ name$(I%)
270     UNTIL name$(I%)="***"
275 C%=I%-1
280 ENDPROC
290
300 DEF PROCsort(C%)
320 REPEAT
330     swaps%=0
340     FOR I%=1 TO C%-1
350       IF name$(I%)>name$(I%+1)THEN PROCswap
360       NEXT I%
365       C%=C%-1
370     UNTIL swaps%=0
380 ENDPROC
390
400 DEF PROCswap
410 keep$=name$(I%)
420 name$(I%)=name$(I%+1)
430 name$(I%+1)=keep$
440 swaps%=swaps%+1
450 ENDPROC
460
470 DEF PROCdisplay(C%)
480 FOR I%=1 TO C%
490     PRINT name$(I%)
500     NEXT I%
510 ENDPROC
520
530 DATA MIKE,ANN,JOHN,WILF,CHRIS,TOM
1000 DATA ***
```

Fig. 6.10 The alphabetical sort program rewritten with integer variables and diminishing pass through the DATA (line 365 C% = C% − 1, where C% sets the number of records to be examined). Note that more names must be added, and the last 'name' must be the dummy ***.

The timings for this bubble sort for sorting 100 names into alphabetical order can therefore be summarised as follows:

Features	Time in seconds
Floating point variables	56.77
Integer variables	34.82
Integer variables with diminishing pass through the DATA	26.52

It is suggested that the reader should enter the program shown in Fig. 6.10 and test it with various amounts of DATA.

Of course, we would not wish to go through the previous tortuous route every time we wanted to write a program involving sorting. Now that we have a procedure which works it may be simply 'slotted' into a convenient place in a subsequent modular program. This is one advantage of a true module, with no branches into or out of it other than the procedure call. A routine which contained numerous GOTOs to other parts of the program could not be inserted as a complete unit into another program.

One advantage of the bubble sort is that if the names are already partially sorted in their initial state then the number of passes through the data will be correspondingly reduced. However, if a word is a long way from its final destination, the process of 'bubbling' is rather laborious. Suppose in a list of 100 names, the word ABLE was at the bottom, whereas its true position in the sorted list should be at the top. In order to move it to its final destination, we need to pass through the data many times comparing and swapping the pairs of names. The name ABLE will move up the list only one position on each pass through the data.

The Shell sort

This method produces a much faster sort by dividing the list into two halves and comparing names in the bottom half with those in the corresponding position in the top half. In this way a name like ABLE would move immediately into the top half of the list during the first pass through the data. Subsequent passes through the names make comparisons across successively smaller spans. For example, taking an unrealistically small sample of 8 names, we would compare (and swap if necessary) names 5 and 1, 6 and 2, 7 and 3, and 8 and 4. (If ABLE started at position 8, it would arrive in the top half after only one pass through the data.)

During the next pass we halve the span of comparison and examine names 3 and 1, 4 and 2, 5 and 3 etc. The final pass compares names 2 with 1, 3 and 2 etc., after which the names will be in order.

An important feature with this method is that if, say, we had swapped name 8 with name 6, we must then compare the new name 6 with name 4. If 6 and 4 are swapped then the new name 4 must be compared with name 2 and swapped, if necessary.

The essential differences between the Shell and Bubble sorts are therefore:

1 The Shell sort compares names across a 'span' initially equal to half of the data. Thus

56 Sorting Data

a word out of position immediately moves a distance equal to half of the table—not 'bubbling' up one position at a time.

2   Repeated passes through the names, each time reducing the span by a factor of 2, together with retrospective comparisons up the list, result in a finally sorted list.

This is a complex method, but the basic routine can be demonstrated with the set of six names used in the previous section—a ridiculous number compared with the hundreds needed to justify the use of a computer.

In this example, the span of comparison is reduced using DIV 2, the BBC BASIC statement which performs division ignoring any remainder. Thus 3 DIV 2 = 1.

1st PASS: SPAN OF COMPARISON = (6 DIV 2) = 3

```
              SMITH ─┐      SMITH         SMITH
              BROWN  │      BROWN─┐       ABLE
              JONES  │      JONES  │      JONES ─┐
              WALKER─┘      WALKER │      WALKER │
              ABLE          ABLE ──┘      BROWN  │
              BONNER        BONNER        BONNER─┘
```

2nd PASS: SPAN OF COMPARISON = (3 DIV 2) = 1

```
SMITH─┐    ABLE         ABLE ─┐    ABLE         ABLE         ABLE
ABLE ─┘    SMITH ─┐     BONNER┘    BONNER       BONNER       BONNER
BONNER     BONNER─┘     SMITH      SMITH─┐      SMITH        SMITH ─┐
WALKER     WALKER       WALKER     WALKER┘      WALKER─┐     BROWN─┘
BROWN      BROWN        BROWN      BROWN        BROWN ─┘     WALKER
JONES      JONES        JONES      JONES        JONES        JONES
```

2nd PASS CONTINUED

```
ABLE        ABLE        ABLE        ABLE
BONNER─┐    BONNER      BONNER      BONNER
BROWN ─┘    BROWN       BROWN       BROWN─┐
SMITH       SMITH       SMITH ─┐    JONES─┘
WALKER      WALKER─┐    JONES ─┘    SMITH
JONES       JONES ─┘    WALKER      WALKER
```

KEY   ─ ─┐ names compared but
           ─ ─┘ not swapped

           ───┐ names compared and
           ───┘ swapped

It can be seen that only two passes through the data are needed, (the bubble sort required 5). Note the speed with which ABLE moves up the table.

The second pass requires some retrospective comparisons to be made and this is best explained by an example. After WALKER and BROWN have been exchanged, BROWN is then compared with the next name one span up the table. In this case BROWN is compared with SMITH and a further swap takes place. In its new position, BROWN must again be compared with the name one span above it, so the comparison is made with BONNER. This time no exchange is necessary so the Shell sort resumes the pass through the data with the next two names which were due to be compared before the retrospective swaps took place. In this example WALKER is compared with JONES and initiates another series of retrospective comparisons.

In practice, of course, we would sort far more than the six names used here to demonstrate the process. With 100 names, for example, the initial span of 50 names means that the names perform some very large jumps up and down the list.

The Shell sort

The Shell sort program is given in Fig. 6.11 with the corresponding flow diagram in Fig. 6.12.

```
  10 DIM name$(110)
  20 TIME=0
  30
  40 PROCread
  50
  60 PROCsort
  70
  80 PROCdisplay
  90
 100 PRINT "TIME "TIME/100" SECS"
 110 END
 120
 130 DEF PROCread
 140 I%=0
 150 REPEAT
 160   I%=I%+1
 170   READ name$(I%)
 180   UNTIL name$(I%)="***"
 190 C%=I%-1
 200 ENDPROC
 210
 220 DEF PROCsort
 230 span=C% DIV 2
 240 REPEAT
 250   IFspan<1 THEN 300
 260   FOR I%=span+1 TO C%
 270     PROCtest(I%,I%-span)
 280     NEXTI%
 290   span=span DIV 2
 300   UNTIL span<1
 310 ENDPROC
 320
 330 DEF PROCtest(m,n)
 340 IF n<0 THEN ENDPROC
 350 IFname$(m)>name$(n) THEN ENDPROC
 360 PROCswap(m,n): PROCtest(n,n-span)
 370 ENDPROC
 380
 390 DEF PROCswap(m,n)
 400 keep$=name$(m)
 410 name$(m)=name$(n)
 420 name$(n)=keep$
 430 ENDPROC
 440
 450 DEF PROCdisplay
 460 FOR I%=1 TO C%
 470   PRINT name$(I%)" ";
 480   NEXT I%
 490 ENDPROC
 500
 510 DATA MIKE,ANN,JOHN,WILF,CHRIS,TOM
1000 DATA ***
```

Fig. 6.11 The Shell sort. Additional names are added by extending the DATA statements. *** must terminate the DATA.

58 *Sorting Data*

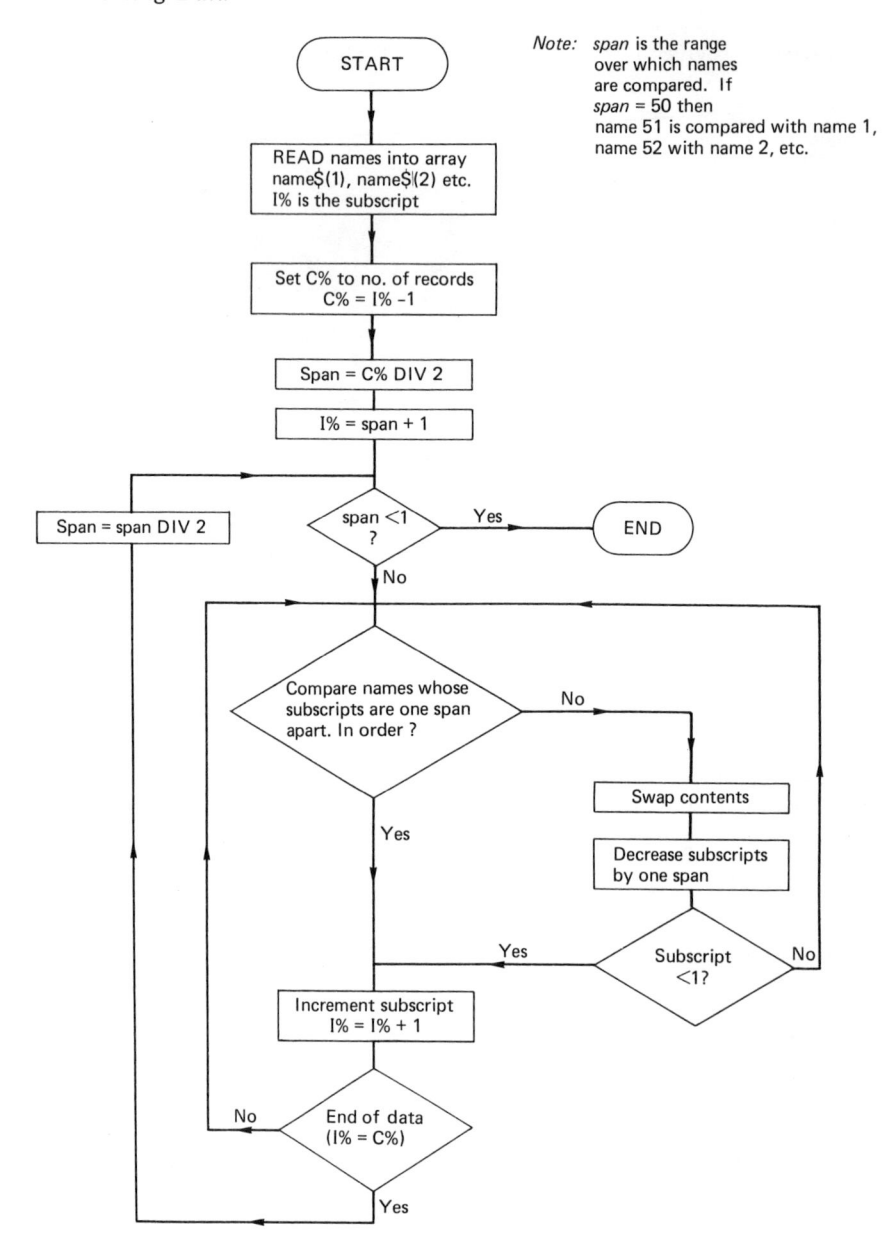

Fig. 6.12 Flow diagram for the Shell sort

The Shell sort program in detail

The program (Fig. 6.11) reads the data in the same way as the previous 'bubble' sort program. PROCsort, however, is very different. First the set of names is divided into two halves using *span* = C% DIV 2, where *span* is the range over which names are to be compared. C% is the total number of names read into the array name$(I%). DIV 2 ensures that if an odd number of names are read, only the integer part of the answer is used. So that if 101 names were read, the *span* would be 101 DIV 2 i.e. 50. In this case, the program would compare word 51 with 1, word 52 with 2 etc. and finally 101 with 51. The alphabetical comparisons are made in repeated passes through the data in the REPEAT ... UNTIL loop (lines 240 to 300 inclusive). The comparisons are made in PROCtest which uses the familiar PROCswap as employed in the previous 'bubble' sort program. After each pass through the data, the span of comparison is halved by the line

```
290 span = span DIV 2
```

Finally, the sorting is completed when the span is less than 1, i.e. adjacent pairs have been compared and swapped if necessary. To streamline the passing of parameters from PROCsort to PROCtest and PROCswap, the unwieldy I% and (I% – span) are passed to the neater variable names *m* and *n*.

The statement PROCtest (n, n – *span*) plays a major part in the Shell sort. This executes the retrospective comparison back up the list. Note also that this is an example of the strange phenomenon of a procedure calling itself.

Comparing the Bubble and Shell sorts

We can easily modify the two programs to find out the number of operations involved in sorting the same 100 names by the Shell and Bubble sort methods. All we need is to place a few counters in appropriate places and then to print their values at the end of each sort. The counters must be inserted in both the Bubble sort (Fig. 6.10) and the Shell sort (Fig. 6.11).

First we need to compare the number of passes through the data. This can be achieved by inserting:

```
passes = passes + 1
```

This statement should go immediately after REPEAT in DEF PROCsort (Figs 6.10 and 6.11).

Second, we need to know the total number of comparisons made (these comparisons may or may not lead to an exchange).

```
comparisons = comparisons + 1
```

should be inserted immediately after the statement DEF PROCtest(m,n) in the Shell sort (Fig. 6.11) and immediately after the FOR ... statement in DEF PROCsort in the Bubble sort (Fig. 6.10).

Finally, we need the number of exchanges (swaps) made in sorting 100 names. The statement:

```
exchanges = exchanges + 1
```

inserted immediately after DEF PROCswap, in both programs, should suffice.

The counters may be displayed by inserting, immediately before the END statement:

```
PRINT "PASSES "passes,"COMPARISONS "comparisons,"EXCHANGES "
exchanges
```

60 *Sorting Data*

When the counters were inserted in the Bubble sort and Shell sort programs, using the same set of 100 names, the results were as follows:

Sorting of 100 names	Type of sort	
	Bubble	Shell
No. of passes through the data	89	6
No. of comparisons	4895	911
No. of exchanges	2414	456
Time to sort the same set of 100 names (seconds)	26.52	11.37

Obviously the figures cannot be regarded as absolute since the performance of the two methods is affected by the initial state of 'sortedness' of the data.

The times to sort 100 names were obtained before the counters were inserted, as these add considerably to the times.

Summary

- The sort routine can form an independent procedure or module for assembly when 'building' future programs from a series of existing blocks.
- The Bubble sort provides a simple but relatively slow method of sorting words into alphabetical order (or sorting numbers into numerical order).
- The Shell sort, while rather more complex to program and understand, is a fast method and suitable for the typical micro user wishing to sort a few hundred items.

Although there are many other types of sort, the methods just described are adequate for the small business user/administrator using a microcomputer.

The next chapter will combine the main elements covered so far i.e. the READ, DISPLAY, SEARCH and SORT modules, into a fully menu-driven, modular program to do a useful piece of work.

7

Developing a Menu-Driven Program

So far we have covered several of the main operations in data processing, such as reading, displaying, searching and sorting. Let us now try to assemble these into a complete and useful program. For simplicity we will base the program around a personal telephone directory, which might also be suitable for a small business regularly contacting perhaps 100 customers.

It is not suggested that every time you need a telephone number you switch on the computer and load and search a cassette tape! Even in an office using machines equipped with floppy disks constantly 'powered up' it would hardly be worthwhile by the time the correct disk was located and loaded. No, the advantages of the microcomputer would be its ability to produce, periodically, a printed list, on paper, which contained the latest information. The benefits of this method over existing manual systems are that such information is:

1 Easy to update (i.e. amend, delete, extend).
2 Automatically sorted into the required order.

Of course, the telephone directory is just a simple example—the same basic design may be extended to produce programs handling more complex records which justify the use of a computer more obviously. The idea at this stage is to produce a standard program format; a basic skeleton onto which various modules may be assembled.

Before writing the BASIC code, let us decide what we want the program to do.

1 DATA
This will be the name and telephone number, stored in *name$* and *phone$*. We will need to use these as array variables for approximately 100 records, so the program must be dimensioned. We will allow a further 20 records for expansion. The required statement is therefore:

`100 DIM name$(120),phone$(120)`

The reader may prefer to store both name and number in a single store location, such as *name$(X)*, in which case a typical record might contain

"JOHN BROWN 0302 546", stored say, in *name$(19)*.

This might be quite practical in the case of the telephone program with its simple records. However, the use of these compound fields makes searching or sorting more difficult. For instance, it would not be easy to search for a telephone number, or to sort the names into

62 Developing a Menu-driven Program

alphabetical order. To manipulate these parts of strings it would be necessary to indulge in 'string slicing', using RIGHT$,LEFT$ and MID$.

Typically a large record may consist of 5 or 10 fields, and require searching for any combination of them. Further, the use of variable length fields would make the programming of RIGHT$,LEFT$ and MID$ more complex.

We will therefore use the separate variables *name$(X)* and *phone$(X)* for the two separate fields of name and number, in preparation for programming more complex records each containing many fields.

2 PROCESS

To process this data we will only be concerned with sorting into alphabetical order, or searching for a record containing either a particular name or a particular number. (No meaningful calculation can be carried out on telephone numbers so the numbers are stored in *phone$(X)* rather than numeric store *phone(X)*.)

3 OUTPUT

We will include options to display the entire file or display an individual record. This will be achieved by PROCprint to display an individual record; PROCprint may also be called from other procedures e.g. by enclosing in a FOR ... NEXT loop to form PROCdisplay.

Directing output to paper

Printed output can be obtained on paper by holding down the control key, CTRL, and briefly depressing key B prior to running the program. Similarly the output to the printer may be discontinued by holding down CTRL with brief depression of key C. Alternatively, the printer may be opened by the statement VDU2 and closed by the statement VDU3 inserted at suitable places within the program.

Now let us plan the modules in the form of a block diagram before 'coding', i.e. translating the modules into BASIC. The plan is shown in Fig. 7.1.

Note that after completion of each of the four main optional procedures PROCdisplay, PROCname, PROCnumber and PROCsort, the user is returned to the menu. So to produce a sorted list we will carry out PROCsort, which will sort into alphabetical order but will not include any printing. To display or print the fully sorted list after executing PROCsort, we return to the menu and type option 1 to execute PROCdisplay. This will print the sorted records.

With a large number of records to sort, the computer may appear to be doing nothing, or to have crashed. For this reason I have included the note "SORTING IN PROGRESS" at lines 650 and 660 (CH$(141) produces double height letters if the line is repeated).

Now that we have planned the broad outline of the program it is just a case of translating into BASIC code. One further problem must be resolved, however, concerned with the swap routine. The previous example for 100 names was simple since the contents of only one array (*name$(X)*) needed to be interchanged.

Imagine that we are comparing *name$(19)* with *name$(20)* and their contents are interchanged during the bubble sort. In the telephone program now being planned not only will there be a *name$(19)* but also an associated *phone$(19)*. If we only swap array *name$(X)* then the contents of *phone$(X)* will be associated with the wrong name. It is therefore necessary in the bubble sort to make sure that when a swap takes place on the particular field used for sorting, then every associated field in that record must also be

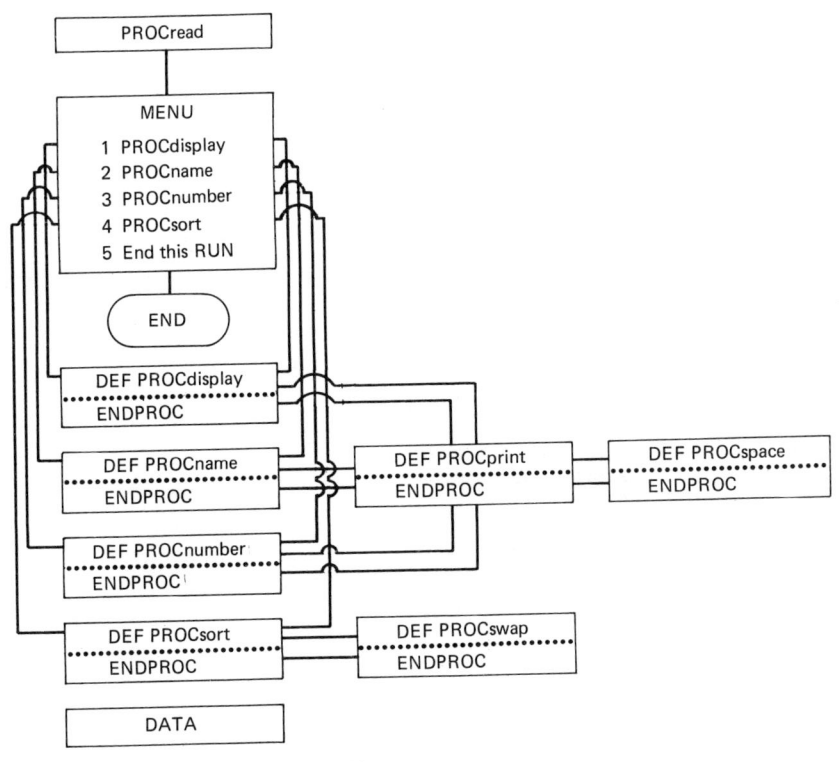

```
                    ┌──────────────┐
                    │   PROCread   │
                    └──────┬───────┘
                    ┌──────┴───────┐
                    │     MENU     │
                    │ 1 PROCdisplay│
                    │ 2 PROCname   │
                    │ 3 PROCnumber │
                    │ 4 PROCsort   │
                    │ 5 End this RUN│
                    └──────┬───────┘
                        ( END )
```

Fig. 7.1 The modules of a menu driven program

swapped. A further example might consist of records each having four fields: name, street, town, postcode. If the names are swapped, then the other 3 fields consisting of street, town and postcode must be swapped simultaneously, to keep the original records intact.

Returning to the telephone directory, a swap routine to exchange both name and number is shown in Fig. 7.2. To retain a copy of *name$(I%)* before it is overwritten we have used store *keep$*; similarly *hold$* preserves a copy of the original contents of store *phone$(I%)*.

```
810 DEF PROCswap
820 keep$=name$(I%)
830 hold$=phone$(I%)
840 name$(I%)=name$(I%+1)
850 phone$(I%)=phone$(I%+1)
860 name$(I%+1)=keep$
870 phone$(I%+1)=hold$
880 swaps%=swaps%+1
890 ENDPROC
```

Fig. 7.2 A swap routine to exchange both name and telephone number

We have now covered all of the necessary steps to 'build' the complete program (Fig. 7.3). There is very little new programming; apart from the swap routine, most of the coding can be copied from the car program described earlier.

Developing a Menu-driven Program

```
100   DIM name$(110),phone$(110)
110
120   PROCread
130
140   REPEAT
150     PROCmenu
160     IF option=1 THEN PROCdisplay(C%)
170     IF option=2 THEN PROCname(C%)
180     IF option=3 THEN PROCnumber(C%)
190     IF option=4 THEN PROCsort(C%)
200     UNTIL option=5
210   END
220
230   DEF PROCmenu
240   CLS
250   PRINT TAB(8,8);"1:Display the file"
260   PRINT TAB(8,10);"2:Search for a name"
270   PRINT TAB(8,12);"3:Search for a number"
280   PRINT TAB(8,14);"4:Sort into order"
290   PRINT TAB(8,16);"5:End"
300   option=GET-48
310   ENDPROC
320
330   DEF PROCread
340   I%=0
350   REPEAT
360     I%=I%+1
370     READ name$(I%),phone$(I%)
380     UNTIL name$(I%)="***"
390   C%=I%-1
400   ENDPROC
410   DEF PROCdisplay(C%)
420   FOR N%=1 TO C%
430     PROCprint
440     NEXT N%
450   ENDPROC
460
470   DEF PROCname(C%)
480   CLS:PRINT''''''
490   INPUT"ENTER THE NAME "search$
500   FOR N%=1 TO C%
510     IF name$(N%)=search$ THEN PROCprint
520     NEXT N%
530   ENDPROC
540
550   DEF PROCnumber(C%)
560   CLS:PRINT''''''
570   INPUT"ENTER THE NUMBER "number$
580   FOR N%=1 TO C%
590     IF phone$(N%)=number$ THEN PROCprint
600     NEXT N%
610   ENDPROC
620
630   DEF PROCsort(C%)
640   CLS
650   PRINTTAB(8,10);CHR$(141)"SORTING IN PROGRESS"
660   PRINTTAB(8,11);CHR$(141)"SORTING IN PROGRESS"
670   REPEAT
```

```
 680      swaps%=0
 690      FOR I%=1 TO C%-1
 700        IF name$(I%)>name$(I%+1) THEN PROCswap
 710      NEXT I%
 720      C%=C%-1
 730    UNTIL swaps%=0
 740    CLS
 750    PRINT TAB(7,8);"Sorting Complete."
 760    PRINT TAB(7,10);"Please return to the Menu"
 770    PRINT TAB(7,12);"and Display the file"
 780    PROCspace
 790    ENDPROC
 800
 810    DEF PROCswap
 820    keep$=name$(I%)
 830    hold$=phone$(I%)
 840    name$(I%)=name$(I%+1)
 850    phone$(I%)=phone$(I%+1)
 860    name$(I%+1)=keep$
 870    phone$(I%+1)=hold$
 880    swaps%=swaps%+1
 890    ENDPROC
 900
 910    DEF PROCprint
 920    CLS:PRINT'''''
 930    PRINT TAB(8,5);"NAME : ";name$(N%)
 940    PRINT TAB(8,8);"TEL. : ";phone$(N%)
 950    PROCspace
 960    ENDPROC
 970
 980    DEF PROCspace
 990    PRINT''''';TAB(6);"Press Space";
1000    PRINT" to Continue"
1010    REPEAT UNTIL GET=32
1020    ENDPROC
1030
1040    DATA JILL,060954
1050    DATA JOHN,841695
1060    DATA ***,***
```

Fig. 7.3 A menu-driven program to permit the handling of a telephone directory, with options to search and sort

This program may now be entered and RUN. The user should enter the DATA at line 1040 onwards, remembering always to finish the DATA with a complete 'dummy' record ***, ***.

Obviously, the intention with this example was to give a format for larger programs which the user may wish to write. More records can be added provided the DIM statement at line 100 is modified. For more complex records with perhaps 5 fields per record instead of two, as in this example, it will be necessary to extend the list of variables. It will also be necessary to modify the swap procedure to include the required number of holding stores.

When this program was written, two search options were included—to search for a name or search for a number. To make this easier to follow, these options were programmed as separate procedures, PROCname and PROCnumber. It would have been possible to carry out this search (inputting either a name or a number) in one procedure.

66 *Developing a Menu-driven Program*

This would be achieved by setting up the pass through the DATA in the usual way in a FOR ... NEXT loop. However, since we may have INPUT *either* a name *or* a number we test each record as follows:

```
510 IF name$(N%) = search$ THEN PROCprint

520 IF phone$(N%)= search$ THEN PROCprint
```

This would enable the searching for either name or number to be carried out in a single search procedure as follows:

```
470 DEF PROCsearch
480 CLS:PRINT''''
490 INPUT"ENTER SEARCH FIELD"search$
500 FOR N%=1 TO C%
510    IF name$(N)%=search$ THEN PROCprint
520    IF phone$(N)%=search$ THEN PROCprint
530    NEXT N%
540 ENDPROC
```

Fig. 7.4 Searching on either of two fields, name or telephone number

The above procedure would be inserted in the program Fig. 7.3 to replace both PROCname and PROCnumber. The menu would also need to be modified to allow for the reduced number of options.

A further modification would be to insert

```
90 ON ERROR GOTO 140
```

This line would ensure that should an error occur during the running of the program the user will be returned to the menu. This will also happen if ESCAPE is pressed. Line 90 should only be inserted *after* the program has been thoroughly tested and debugged as this modification has the effect of suppressing error messages helpful in the development of the program.

When the program has been entered it should first be saved (*before* running at all).

It should then be tested and corrected if necessary with a small set of data.

Finally, the full set of data should be entered and the program saved on tape or disk.

Out of data error

Initial testing of a program frequently produces an error message of the type 'Out of data at 370' where line 370 is the READ statement assigning the DATA into the arrays. Invariably this error is caused by incorrect DATA as follows:

- Incomplete records (i.e. not enough fields per record).
- Commas placed within a **field** or at the end of a statement thereby creating additional incorrect fields. This causes fields to be shunted into the next available record. (If a comma is needed within a field then the entire field should be enclosed in inverted commas.)

    e.g. "26,LONDON RD,READING"

- Failure to press RETURN at the end of a statement, causing **concatenation**, (sticking together) of two statements and reducing the number of effective records.

- Failure to include dummy DATA consisting of one complete record with the required number of fields.

    e.g. `10000 DATA ***,***`

Updating the program file

DATA stored in this way, attached to the end of a program, is known as a **program file** (as opposed to the separate DATA files discussed later).

The program file would be saved on tape or disk for future use. If necessary, the file could be updated as follows:

1. LOAD and LIST the program.
2. **Amend** a record by retyping the required statement(s), (or by copying and altering where necessary).
3. **Insert** a record by typing a DATA statement with a suitable intermediate line number.
4. **Append** a record by typing a DATA statement with the next available line number (remembering to conclude the DATA with the end-of-DATA marker).
5. **Delete** a record by entering the line number of the record to be deleted and pressing RETURN.

When the DATA has been modified in this way, the updated file exists only in the computer's **volatile** memory. To make a **permanent** copy of the new file, the program must now be reSAVED.

For an important file it is obviously worth making at least one duplicate back-up copy on another tape or diskette.

Now that we have covered one complete program which embraces many of the basic operations, the next section extends the work to include a more useful variable list. This will include records containing five general purpose fields, with the options to search and sort as previously demonstrated in the telephone program.

8

Developing a General Purpose Data Handling Program

The previous chapter gave a program to perform a *specific* task i.e. the recording, searching and updating of a telephone directory. In this section we will develop a general purpose program which it is hoped can be adapted by the reader to a variety of applications. We will extend the variable list to 5, which is adequate for many purposes—for example, a name and address file.

The ability of BBC BASIC to handle strings each of more than 200 characters, means that some very useful records may be handled using 5 strings or variables per record. Alternatively, it is hoped that the reader may use this program as a model on which to base much larger records, containing, say, 10 fields per record.

We will include the following options:

1   Display the entire file (rather like Ceefax, but under the control of the space bar). The BBC micro user can insert colour to simulate the Teletext mode more accurately, using mode 7, to produce some very pleasing results.
2   Search for any one of the five fields.
3   Sort into alphabetical order using a key field (programmed as field 1).

The actual programming requires very little original work: it is simply necessary to expand the telephone program of Chapter 7 to cater for 5 fields stored in 5 arrays, rather than the 2 used in the telephone directory. So *name$(X)* and *phone$(X)* must be replaced throughout by a set of 5 variables. As we are producing a general purpose program we will call these *field1$(X), field2$(X), field3$(X), field4$(X)* and *field5$(X)*.

If the user decides to write a specific program, then the names *field1$(X), field2$(X)* etc. might be replaced by meaningful names such as

name$(X)

street$(X)

town$(X)

county$(X)

tel$(X)

Note that X is simply the subscript which will be assigned to the DATA during any READ operations in a FOR ... NEXT or REPEAT ... UNTIL loop. For 100 records X will be replaced by 1,2,3 ..... 100.

Similarly, although this example uses 5 string variables, the reader could easily omit the $ in order to store numeric data for calculation purposes.

Most of the procedures, then, require little modification from those in the telephone program other than extending the variable list e.g. PROCread now requires

```
350 READ field$(I%),field2$(I%),field3$(I%)

360 READ field4$(I%),field5$(I%)
```

The menu, PROCdisplay and PROCsort are basically the same, while PROCswap must now be extended to swap all five fields instead of only two. PROCspace, of course, is identical, and this illustrates the adapability of procedures—future programming is really assembling existing procedures as modules or blocks.

It is better to avoid branching to line numbers as in earlier forms of BASIC which used GOTO and GOSUB statements. Complete procedures can be inserted as independent modules. It is then only a case of extending the menu and the variable lists to suit the application. This idea is very similar to the modern manufacturing design used for washing machines, televisions, etc. Instead of a repair engineer having to manipulate a tangled maze of wires to correct a fault, he simply 'plugs in' a replacement module. The old fashioned forms of BASIC which resulted in 'spaghetti' caused by too many GOTOs were analogous to the early electrical circuits.

Similarly with independent procedures accessed only by PROC calls, faults can be identified and corrected more easily.

The complete program is shown in Fig. 8.1. It is suggested that the reader enters this program and saves it on disk or tape. Any type of DATA may be used provided there are 5 fields per record. After the program, several examples are given of the types of record and corresponding DATA statements, which are acceptable to the program. Remember, however, that the program will not work unless the DATA is terminated by a statement such as

```
10000 DATA ***,***,***,***,***
```

```
  90   ON ERROR GOTO 160
 100   DIM field1$(110),field2$(110)
 110   DIM field3$(110),field4$(110)
 120   DIM field5$(110)
 130
 140   PROCread
 150
 160   REPEAT
 170      PROCmenu
 180      IF option=1 THEN PROCdisplay(C%)
 190      IF option=2 THEN PROCsearch(C%)
 200      IF option=3 THEN PROCsort(C%)
 210      UNTIL option=4
 220   END
 230
 240   DEF PROCmenu
 250   CLS
 260   PRINT TAB(8,8);"1:Display the File"
 270   PRINT TAB(8,10);"2:Search for a Field"
```

Fig 8.1 A general purpose data handling program, with options to
- display the whole file
- search for any field
- sort on the key field

```
280    PRINT TAB(8,12);"3:Alphasort"
290    PRINT TAB(8,14);"4:End this RUN"
300    option=GET-48
310    ENDPROC
320
330    DEF PROCread
340    I%=0
350    REPEAT
360      I%=I%+1
370      READ field1$(I%),field2$(I%)
380      READ field3$(I%),field4$(I%)
390      READ field5$(I%)
400      UNTIL field1$(I%)="***"
410    C%=I%-1
420    ENDPROC
430
440    DEF PROCdisplay(C%)
450    FOR N%=1 TO C%
460      PROCprint
470      NEXT N%
480    ENDPROC
490
500    DEF PROCsearch(C%)
510    CLS:PRINT''''''
520    INPUT"ENTER THE SEARCH FIELD "search$
530    FOR N%=1 TO C%
540      IF field1$(N%)=search$ THEN PROCprint
550      IF field2$(N%)=search$ THEN PROCprint
560      IF field3$(N%)=search$ THEN PROCprint
570      IF field4$(N%)=search$ THEN PROCprint
580      IF field5$(N%)=search$ THEN PROCprint
590      NEXT N%
600    ENDPROC
610
620    DEF PROCsort(C%)
630    CLS
640    PRINT TAB(8,10);CHR$(141)"SORTING IN PROGRESS"
650    PRINT TAB(8,11);CHR$(141)"SORTING IN PROGRESS"
660    REPEAT
670      swaps%=0
680      FOR I%=1 TO C%-1
690        IF field1$(I%)>field1$(I%+1)THEN PROCswap
700      NEXT I%
710      C%=C%-1
720      UNTIL swaps%=0
730    CLS
740    PRINT TAB(7,8);"Sorting Complete."
750    PRINT TAB(7,10);"Please return to the Menu"
760    PRINT TAB(7,12);"and Display the file"
770    PROCspace
780    ENDPROC
790
800    DEF PROCswap
810    store1$=field1$(I%)
820    store2$=field2$(I%)
830    store3$=field3$(I%)
```

Fig. 8.1 (continued)

```
 840   store4$=field4$(I%)
 850   store5$=field5$(I%)
 860   field1$(I%)=field1$(I%+1)
 870   field2$(I%)=field2$(I%+1)
 880   field3$(I%)=field3$(I%+1)
 890   field4$(I%)=field4$(I%+1)
 900   field5$(I%)=field5$(I%+1)
 910   field1$(I%+1)=store1$
 920   field2$(I%+1)=store2$
 930   field3$(I%+1)=store3$
 940   field4$(I%+1)=store4$
 950   field5$(I%+1)=store5$
 960   swaps%=swaps%+1
 970   ENDPROC
 980
 990   DEF PROCprint
1000   CLS
1010   PRINT TAB(8,5);field1$(N%)
1020 PRINT TAB(8,7);field2$(N%)
1030 PRINT TAB(8,9);field3$(N%)
1040 PRINT TAB(8,11);field4$(N%)
1050 PRINT TAB(8,13);field5$(N%)
1060   PROCspace
1070   ENDPROC
1080
1090   DEF PROCspace
1100   PRINT'''''';TAB(6);"Press space";
1110   PRINT " to continue"
1120   REPEAT UNTIL GET=32
1130   ENDPROC
1140
1150   DATA MORRIS,MINOR,RED,FAIR,3500
1160   DATA FORD,ESCORT,GREEN,GOOD,2100
1170   DATA AUSTIN,MINI,BLUE,V.GOOD,1950
1180   DATA ***,***,***,***,***
```

Fig. 8.1 (continued)

The records should be added from line 1150 onwards. Any number of records may be added, subject to the following limitations:

- the arguments (numbers) in the DIM statements,
- the available memory,
- the presence of the End of DATA dummy record,

    DATA ***,***,***,***,***

The DATA

This program will accept a wide variety of DATA, provided it can be arranged into 5 fields per record — otherwise the variable list must be extended. However, since one string may be approximately 240 characters long, we have considerable potential with this format.

72 Developing a General Purpose Data Handling Program

Some suitable examples and their corresponding DATA statements are as follows:

Example 1

FIELD 1	FORD
FIELD 2	ESCORT
FIELD 3	RED
FIELD 4	1983
FIELD 5	A256LAP

One record. Field 1 is the key field used in alphabetical **sorting**. Any of the five fields may be entered as **search** fields.

```
1000 DATA FORD,ESCORT,RED,1983,A256LAP
```

Note that the complete file would consist of a large number of similar DATA statements.

Example 2

FIELD 1	HAFFLINGER
FIELD 2	TYROLESE
FIELD 3	14 HANDS
FIELD 4	VERY STRONG
FIELD 5	DARK BAY

```
1000 DATA HAFFLINGER,TYROLESE,14 HANDS,VERY STRONG,DARK BAY
```

Example 3

FIELD 1	GREATER SPOTTED WOODPECKER
FIELD 2	23CM
FIELD 3	PIED,RED UNDERTAIL
FIELD 4	4-7 EGGS
FIELD 5	LARVAE OR WOOD INSECTS

```
1000 DATA GREATER SPOTTED WOODPECKER,23CM
1010 DATA "PIED,RED UNDERTAIL",4-7 EGGS
1020 DATA LARVAE OF WOOD INSECTS
```

Note that field 3 must be enclosed in inverted commas to prevent the comma within the field acting as a field separator. The effect of omitting the inverted commas would be to make field 3 contain PIED and field 4 contain RED UNDERTAIL. LARVAE OF WOOD INSECTS would then become field 1 of the next record.

It would, of course, be quite acceptable to program this record in one DATA statement, as follows:

```
1000 DATA GREATER SPOTTED WOODPECKER,23C
M,"PIED,RED UNDERTAIL",4-7EGGS,LARVAE OF
WOOD INSECTS
```

Provided care is taken to ensure that there are five fields, separated by commas, then this will work correctly. Very long records can, however, become very difficult to check, especially if there are hundreds of records.

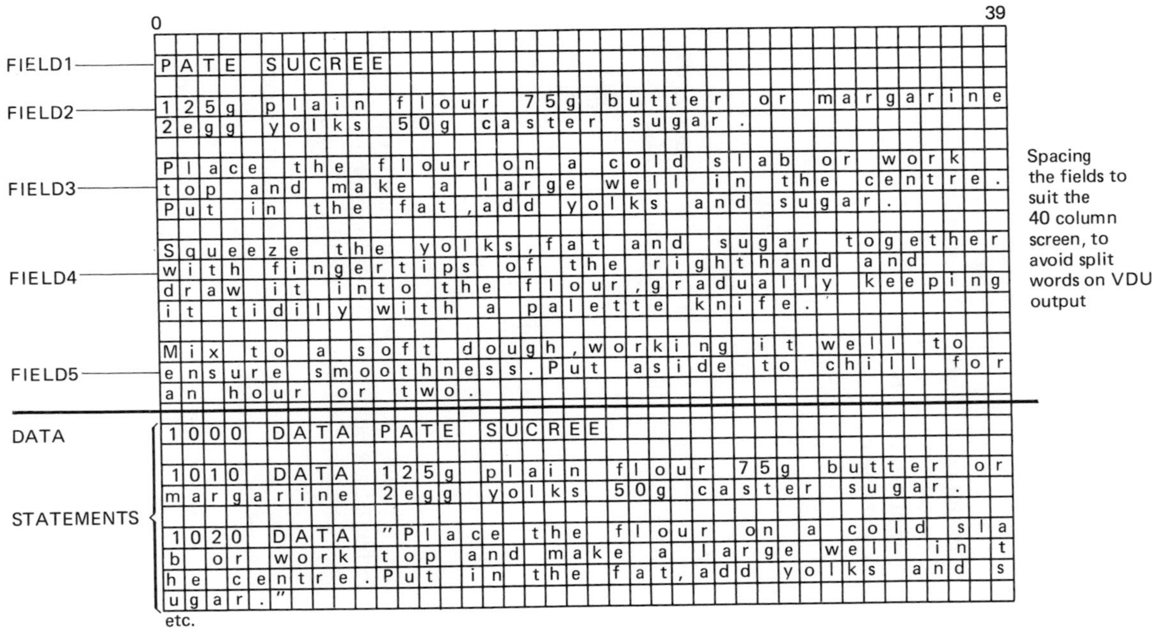

Developing a General Purpose Data Handling Program 73

FIELD1: `PATE SUCREE`

FIELD2: `125g plain flour 75g butter or margarine`

FIELD3: `2egg yolks 50g caster sugar`

FIELD4: `Place the flour, make a well in the centre. work or work together.`

FIELD5: `top and add yolks, fat and sugar and the sugar and butter or margarine`
`Put in the fat, of the yolks, fat working with fingertips slab in the centre.`
`Squeeze the yolks into a paste with fingertips of the flour, gradually working`
`draw in with a palette knife to chill for`
`tidily with a dough, working well to chill for`
`Mix to a soft smooth. Put aside`
`ensure smoothness. Put aside to`
`an hour or two.`

DATA:
```
1000 DATA PATE SUCREE
1010 DATA 125g plain flour, 75g butter or
margarine, 2egg yolks, 50g caster sugar.
1020 DATA "Place the flour, make a well
       or work in the centre. Put
       he centre. Put in the fat, add yolks
       ugar. etc.
```

STATEMENTS

Fig. 8.2 Large data fields. A sample record containing five fields. Each field can extend to approximately 240 characters. Field 1 is the key field, used for searching and sorting. The inverted commas are necessary since field 3 includes commas within its data.

Spacing the fields to suit the 40 column screen, to avoid split words on VDU output

Very long fields

As stated earlier, it is possible for one field to be over 200 characters long, up to a maximum of approximately 240 characters (approximately 1K or 1024 characters on the Master Series). This enables considerable amounts of text to be entered, while obviously making the idea of searching for an individual field rather irrelevant. In this case, it might be possible to enter a short name as the **key field** for searching or sorting.

In order to avoid splitting words at the end of a line, it may be helpful to plan the fields on a 40 column coding sheet to correspond with the screen output. Note that when using the line printer a line width of 80 characters will probably need to be allowed for.

Fig. 8.2 uses a recipe as an example to illustrate the entering of large strings as the 5 fields of a record. First, the 5 fields have been planned on a 40 column coding sheet to adjust the spacing to prevent split words. Then the fields are shown as they would be coded, i.e. as separate DATA statements.

Using the program

Suppose we wished to use the program (Fig. 8.1) to store names and addresses. If alphabetical sorting was required on the person's surname, it would be necessary to enter the records in this form.

FIELD 1	BROWN J.
FIELD 2	39,REGENT ST.
FIELD 3	NEWTON ABBOT
FIELD 4	DEVON
FIELD 5	DE5 8BN

We could enter, say, 100 similar records. Since we have searching on all 5 fields, we could choose option 2 to search the file. If we entered DEVON in response to "ENTER THE SEARCH FIELD", then all residents of that county would be found and displayed on the VDU, or printed on paper.

Similarly, the program could be used for an application such as a newspaper round. It would be possible to enter street as a separate field, and print out all residents of this street.

As written, the program, if asked to find BROWN J. would only print names with that precise spelling. If we want to make the program more flexible, e.g. to print out *all* BROWNS, then we can use LEFT$ in the search module as described earlier.

```
540 IF LEFT$(field1$(N%),LEN(search$))=search$ THEN PROCprint
```

This rather unwieldy expression was covered in more detail earlier in the section on searching, but a plain English description of its function is as follows:

1 The search data is entered and stored in *search$*. This may be a complete name or the first character or group of characters on the left of a name, e.g. B or BROWN or BROWN J.
   The number of characters in this search name will be LEN(*search$*).
2 This search name will be compared with the left-hand portion of every field in the data. The size of the left-hand portion which is considered is determined by the number of characters INPUT to *search$*.

If B is INPUT as the search name, then all fields beginning with B in the DATA will be printed, since only the left-most (1) character will be examined. Similarly, if BROWN is entered, then *every* BROWN will be printed.

Searching on only one field

As written, the program examines all 5 fields in the search routine. The time involved for this, although small, is 5 times as long as when searching on one field. If it is known that only one field is needed for searching, then programming and execution time will be saved if the other searches are omitted. This would be done by only having one line in DEF PROCsearch e.g.

```
IF field1$(N%) = search$ THEN PROCprint
```

At this stage, we should now have the expertise to write a large and useful program.

Further progress in data handling, however, must involve the use of special **data files**, as opposed to the **program files** discussed so far.

The program files, as we have seen, can be used to keep and update records, but they have several major disadvantages which make them unsuitable for commercial applications. These disadvantages may be summarised as follows:

1 In order to append, delete, insert or amend records, it is necessary to LIST the program, type or retype the DATA statement and reSAVE the program. This is programming work and not suitable for an unskilled operator.
2 Every **file** of data must be saved as an integral part of a **program**. This is wasteful of storage space and takes time. One program may be suitable for handling a large number of similar files—it is pointless to have a large program attached to every set of DATA.

The next chapter shows how special data files can be used to overcome the disadvantages of program files.

9

Data Files

The previous chapter mentioned some of the disadvantages of program files, in which every file of data is saved in DATA statements as an integral part of a BASIC program. Such a system can be used to do valuable work provided the user is sufficiently familiar with the program to make the necessary amendments for updating etc. We will now consider the special data files universally used in commercial applications to store large quantities of data quite separate from any program. **Data files** have the following advantages:

- They can be created and updated by an operator in response to simple instructions—no programming knowledge is necessary.
- They are economical of disk/tape storage space since one program may handle many different files.
- The availability of relatively cheap disk drives enables many 'housekeeping' operations to be performed on data files and these operations are just not possible using program files.
- Files can be created which greatly exceed the size of the computer memory.

It must be pointed out that the maximum benefit of data files can only be achieved by the use of a disk storage system. It is possible to handle data files using cassette storage but this cannot be considered as a viable commercial proposition. However, the owner of a cassette system may obtain useful experience in file handling as a preparation for future serious programming when a disk system is available. (I have, in fact, used a cassette-based file for a mailing list of approximately 100 names and addresses which required labels printed at intervals throughout the year. The relatively slow loading of the cassette file still represented a considerable saving of time compared with the retyping of the same set of labels several times a year).

However, the advantages of the disk system are so great that most of this chapter will assume the presence of a disk drive. We will consider both **sequential** and **random** access files; the former can be handled by both cassette and disk systems, the latter are only possible with a disk system. As the name implies, the sequential file must be processed from end to end; a random access file direct allows movement to a required record stored at a known location within a file.

The main advantages of a disk-based system compared with cassette are as follows:

- Programs and files can be SAVED and LOADED with much greater speed, reliability and precision.
- The ability to display almost instantaneously a **catalogue** of all programs and files stored on a particular disk.

- The ability to perform numerous housekeeping operations such as the copying or deletion of programs and files.
- A facility to move a pointer to any point within a data file to permit updating operations.

These complex operations require the presence of an additional ROM chip in the computer—the Disk Filing System (DFS). When files are stored on the disk the DFS keeps a record of the precise location of the beginning of the file. Although more complete details of this process will be found in the User Guide some brief notes may be helpful at this stage.

The Acorn machines use either $3\frac{1}{2}''$ or $5\frac{1}{4}''$ soft-sectored floppy disks and new disks must be prepared for use in a process known as **formatting** (which will also rejuvenate an old disk). Formatting consists of dividing the surface of the disk into a series of concentric **tracks** (either 40 or 80 depending on the type of disk drive unit). A typical 40 track disk is shown in the diagram (Fig. 9.1).

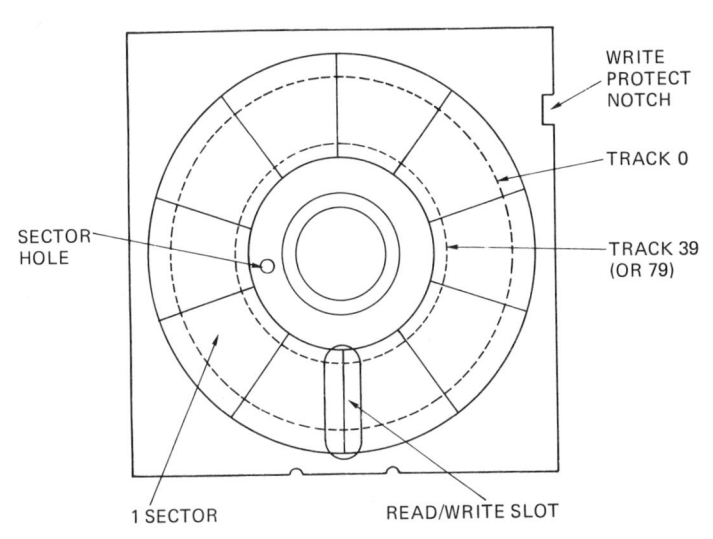

Fig 9.1 The $5\frac{1}{4}''$ floppy disk. Each disk has 10 sectors; each sector contains 256 bytes; a 40 track disk has a capacity of $10 \times 256 \times 40 = 102400$ bytes.

Since one sector contains 256 characters the storage capacity of disks may be calculated as follows:

Tracks	Sectors	Bytes per Sector	Capacity
40	10	256	40 × 10 × 256 = 102400 bytes

Similarly, an 80 track, double-sided disk will have a capacity of $(80 \times 10 \times 256) \times 2 = 409600$ bytes.

The first two sectors of the disk are used for the catalogue, which uses a three digit number to locate the start of a file. The first two digits identify the track (in the range 00–39 or 00–79), and the third digit is the sector (in the range 0–9). This number enables the read/write head to move precisely to the required position on the disk. One DFS disk can hold up to 31 files — in this case files include both **program** and **data files**. The

Advanced Disk Filing System (ADFS) described in the next section permits many more files to be saved on a disk.

At this stage it may be useful to give a condensed list of some of the many commands used with the disk system. In this list the word 'file' is used loosely to mean both program and data files.

Table 9.1 Some of the most frequently used Disk Filing System commands (PROG must be replaced by the name of a particular file)

Command	Function
*ENABLE *FORM40	Used with the presence of Utilities disk, to format or mark out a 40 track disk in tracks and sectors. Also wipes clean and prepares an old disk
SAVE"PROG"	Saves a program file on disk. Any name can be used, to a maximum of 7 letters or characters excluding "#", "*", ".", ":"
LOAD"PROG"	Loads a program file from disk
*CAT(or *.)	Display a catalogue of all programs and data files on the disk
*COMPACT	'Collect' all unused intermediate spaces on the disk and deposit them together at the 'end' to make more space available for new files
*DELETE PROG	Remove the named program/file from the disk.
*ENABLE *BACKUP 00	Make an identical copy of a source disk into a destination disk (by alternately removing and replacing the disks in a single disk drive unit)
*ENABLE *BACKUP 01	Make an identical copy of a source disk in drive 0 onto a destination disk in drive 1 of a dual disk drive unit
*COPY 01 PROG	Copy a program named PROG from a disk in drive 0 to a disk in drive 1
*ACCESS PROG L	Prevents a file from being deleted. Formatting would still delete the file
*ACCESS PROG	Unlocks the previous locked file

It should be noted that when using the SAVE command for a program, if a previous program already exists with that name, the old program will be deleted and replaced by the new.

Obviously Table 9.1 gives only a sample of the many facilities available, but it should be sufficient to enable the beginner to make good use of the disk system. Many more sophisticated commands are available, such as the 'wildcard' facility, which might, for example, be used to delete all files beginning with a certain letter.

The Advanced Disk Filing System (ADFS)

The previous section describes DFS, the standard disk filing system fitted to the BBC Model B. ADFS represents an extended filing system, in which many of the DFS commands remain as a sub-set. However, using double density storage of data on the disk, two major advantages result:

- Storage capacity per disk surface is nearly doubled.
- The limitation of 31 files per disk is removed and replaced by a sophisticated 'hierarchical' structure allowing multiple directories; each directory may contain up to 47 'files'.

The Advanced Disk Filing System (ADFS) 79

ADFS is available as standard on the Acorn Master 128 and the BBC Master Compact (also known as the Olivetti Prodest); DFS is also provided on the Master 128 and transfer between the two systems is achieved by the keyboard commands *ADFS and *DFS. The battery-powered control panel on the Master may be set so that the computer starts up in either DFS or ADFS mode. ADFS may be fitted to the Model B computer by adding the ADFS chip and also the 1770 disk controller chip. On the BBC Model B + , since the 1770 chip is already present, it is only necessary to add the ADFS ROM.

An important point is that the double density ADFS will not read disks prepared in the single density DFS format—hence the ability of the Master to alternate between the two, emulating a model B machine if necessary (to read earlier software). ADFS disks are formatted by inserting the Master Welcome and Utilities disk and entering *AFORM.

With ADFS, storage per side of an 80-track disk is increased from 200K to 320K; instead of one directory containing up to 31 files, multiple directories are now possible, each containing 47 files. A file can be a program, a set of data, and also, in the case of ADFS, a sub-directory. The sub-directories are arranged in a hierarchical structure like a tree or root system. The main root directory is referred to as $ and all directories emanate from it (Fig. 9.2).

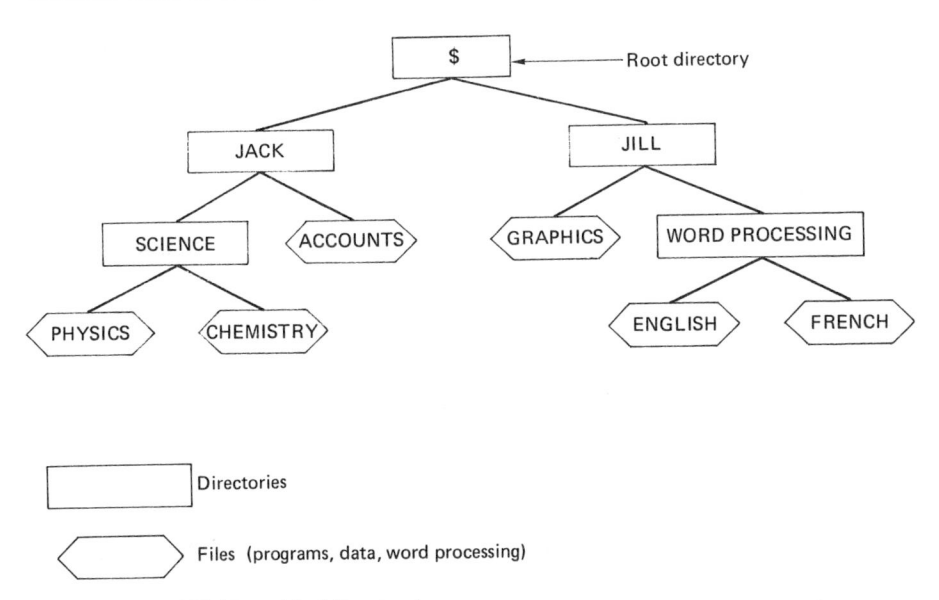

Fig. 9.2 The ADFS hierarchical file structure

Transferring between directories is achieved by the command *DIR⟨Name⟩, where 'name' is the pathname to the required directory. For example, if we are currently in the root directory and wish to move to the SCIENCE directory we would enter *DIR JACK.SCIENCE at the keyboard.

Alternatively we can always use the full pathname starting at the root directory (no matter which directory is currently selected). So the PHYSICS program would be retrieved using LOAD"$.JACK.SCIENCE.PHYSICS".

New directories are created when the command *CDIR ⟨Name⟩ is entered.

The hierarchical file structure is particularly useful on networks, for organising the work of a group of people; one directory may be allocated to the group, with individual directories for each person, (who themselves may create sub-directories.)

Sequential and random access files

In a **sequential** file, the data is saved in a continuous string on the disk or tape. To gain access to a particular record somewhere within the file it is necessary to proceed from the beginning towards the end, until the required record is found. If it is necessary to modify a file then the following procedure is carried out, provided the file does not exceed the available memory.

- Read the whole file from disk or tape back into the memory.
- Modify the file as required.
- Resave on disk or tape.

The **random access** file, possible only with disk systems, uses the **pointer** facility to keep a note of the exact position of the start of each record. This enables individual records or files to be modified on the disk without the need to read the entire file into the computer's memory. Of course, it is necessary to know the pointer position of the required record, or to have some method of calculating it. This implies the need to allocate a fixed number of characters to each field. If, for example, we have 50 characters per record, then the first record will start at pointer position 0, the second at position 50, the third at position 100 i.e. $(n-1) \times 50$, where n is the number of the record.

From this it will be appreciated that the superior performance of random access files is gained at the expense of two disadvantages:

- The need to allocate fixed-length fields will be wasteful of disk space when fields are less than the allocated maximum.
- The programming will be more complicated than an equivalent sequential file.

Sequential files

Writing data to the file

Data is written to a file on a disk or cassette via a 'buffer' in the computer. This is an intermittent process, which occurs either when the buffer is full or an instruction is given to empty the buffer.

To begin writing to a file it is necessary to allocate a channel number for a particular file. This is achieved by the computer, in the OPENOUT statement, e.g.

```
1000 X = OPENOUT"CARS"
```

This causes the computer to allocate a channel number represented by X, to a file called CARS, which is now open to receive data. Any previous file having the same name will be overwritten (unless it had been 'locked' in the manner discussed earlier). Up to 5 such files may be opened simultaneously.

The DATA to be written to the file must be entered into the memory, either by INPUT or READ and DATA statements. For large quantities of DATA there is no point in saving it in DATA statements as well as in a DATA file, so we will consider only the INPUT method.

For simplicity, let us consider a set of 10 names to be stored on file. The sequence of operations is as follows:

1 Open the file to write.

2 Input the DATA.
3 Write the DATA to the file.
4 Close the file

Writing the data to the file is performed by the PRINT# statement (without spaces) and finally the file is closed using the CLOSE# statement.

```
10    X=OPENOUT"NAMES"
20    FOR P=1 TO 10
30       INPUT"ENTER A NAME"N$
40       PRINT#X,N$
50       NEXT
60    CLOSE#X
```

Fig. 9.3 Opening a file to write 10 names

Notice that the channel number, X for this particular file, is used in the PRINT# statement and the CLOSE# statement.

The CLOSE# statement is very important since it has two major functions:

1 Completes the transfer of data from the buffer to the disk i.e. in the likely event that the buffer will not be exactly full.
2 Writes an end-of-file marker—useful when reading a file back from disk to computer memory to detect when reading is complete.

Reading a file from disk to memory

After running the above program, we can then check that a recording of the DATA has in fact been made by reading it back.

We use the OPENIN command to open a file for reading and the INPUT# statement actually transfers the DATA from disk to computer. Although we know in this simple example that there are ten names we will use a test for the end-of-file marker EOF in a REPEAT ... UNTIL loop.

```
10    Y=OPENIN"NAMES"
20    REPEAT
30       INPUT#Y,A$
40       PRINT"NAME "A$
50    UNTIL EOF#Y
60    CLOSE#Y
```

Fig. 9.4 Opening a file to read all of its contents until the detection of the end-of-file marker

Note again that the channel number, Y, while different from that in the write routine, appears in the INPUT#, EOF# and CLOSE# statements. At line 30 the name read from disk is allocated to store A$ in the memory, although any variable name could be used—no variable names are stored with the DATA on the disk.

For the purpose of testing, the two previous programs, Figs 9.3 and 9.4, could be given consecutive line numbers and run as one.

At this stage it may be helpful to make further distinction between program files and data files. Figures 9.3 and 9.4 are programs and for a permanent record must be saved on disk or cassette by the SAVE command with a suitable name. Note that these programs contain no DATA either before or after execution. The DATA, which is entered via the INPUT statements, is written to a separate DATA file on disk by the PRINT# statement—no further saving of DATA being necessary.

82 Data Files

This means that file handling programs are totally independent of the DATA they are handling, and so the same program could be used to create any number of similar DATA files. Slight modification of the example (Fig. 9.3) would be necessary to provide the opportunity to input the file name, i.e.

```
5   INPUT "FILENAME ?"F$

10  X = OPENOUT F$
```

This would enable several similar files to be created, with different names, using the same program.

If the above two lines are added to the program of Fig. 9.3 and RUN, a filename such as FILE1 should be entered. On pressing RETURN some disk activity will be heard. This brief rotation of the disk is the process of writing the header at the front of the file, including the file name. As program execution continues, names are entered to the memory via the INPUT# statements and written on the disk or tape by the PRINT# statements. The latter will not be completed until the CLOSE# statement has been executed.

Similarly if a disk already contained several files we could open the particular one we wanted for reading by specifying the filename as follows:

```
5   INPUT "FILENAME ?"F$

10  Y=OPENIN F$
```

The disk should now contain the file-handling program SAVED in the normal way, and several separate DATA files created by PRINT# statements following an OPENOUT statement. When the catalogue is displayed, the names of the DATA files will appear alongside the names of the program files—the catalogue will make no distinction between them.

Developing a complete program

In order to handle files in a useful way it is necessary to have a program which includes the following modules as options:

1 Create a file.
2 Read a file.
3 Display a file.
4 Update a file.

With a sequential file it will be necessary to read the whole file into an array in order to modify any records. The modified file must then be resaved on disk or tape. Similarly, once in the array in the computer's memory, various other options could be carried out such as sorting or searching as described in previous sections of this book.

We will now confine ourselves to the three fundamental operations mentioned above—Create, Read and Modify. Since we must be able to handle all types of data we will choose an example which includes string, integer and floating point variables—a stock list in a sports shop. As a reminder of the computing jargon, a **file** consisting of five **records** is shown, each record containing three **fields**. (Obviously a practical file would extend to hundreds or thousands of records.)

Developing a complete program 83

	FIELD1	FIELD2	FIELD3
Record No.	Description	Price	No. in Stock
1	Snooker Table	150.95	2
2	Fishing Rod	49.50	5
3	Football Boots	27.10	10
4	Cricket Bat	32.95	9
5	Golf Clubs	215.45	2

Fig. 9.5 A file consisting of 5 records with 3 fields per record

The description field is obviously string data, while the cost, which may later be subject to a calculation, must be stored in a floating point store. The stock will always be whole numbers so this can be stored in an integer variable store. Using meaningful variable names these are

    item$ = description of item
    price   = price of item
    stock% = number in stock

The file will be opened to write using OPENOUT as shown previously, but now that we are using a record containing three fields instead of one we can either write to the disk in one line e.g.

`500 PRINT#X,item$,price,stock%`

Or alternatively, each record may be written in three separate statements:

`510 PRINT#X,item$`

`520 PRINT#X,price`

`530 PRINT#X,stock%`

Similarly, reading back the data from disk (after an OPENIN statement) will require an INPUT# statement such as

`800 INPUT#X,item$,price,stock%`

The reader is reminded that X is an arbitrary variable to which the computer allocates a channel number for a particular file. This variable must be used throughout a particular read or write operation in all statements such as OPENIN, OPENOUT, PRINT#, INPUT#, EOF# etc.

Updating a file

The updating process may involve any of the following operations:

- Modify an existing record by altering one or more fields
- Delete a record.
- Append a new record.

84   Data Files

Modifying an existing record

Sequential files are harder to modify than random access files, since we cannot locate a record with any precision. A method which works is as follows:

1. Read the whole file into an array in the memory.
2. Display the file, showing each record and its subscript. Note the subscript of any record(s) to be modified.
3. Retype the record(s) with the appropriate array subscript.
4. Resave the modified file with a new name (to prevent overwriting the old file—this can be DELETED later if necessary.)

Deleting a record

To delete a record, we simply display the file, note its number then retype it with a dummy name such as "DELETED". When the sequential file is rewritten any records containing the name DELETED will be ignored and the program will skip to the next record.

Appending a record

To do this it is simply necessary to type the record which is to be added to the file using a subscript number which follows immediately that of the last record of the previous file. The file is then rewritten.

Fig. 9.6 shows the structure of a program which can be used to create and maintain a file of data and the listing is given in Fig. 9.7.

The program (Fig. 9.7) can be entered and run as a demonstration using the very limited sportshop DATA given in Fig. 9.5. Alternatively, the reader may prefer to modify the program to create a file of DATA with a different set of variables. In this case it is simply necessary to replace *item$*, *price* and *stock%* by the new variable list.

This program (Fig. 9.7) is only a bare skeleton, on which the reader may build a more elaborate program. It could be made more user-friendly in the following ways:

- Additional instructions and prompts to the user.
- The addition of colour and improved layout using TAB etc.

The program has been written with clarity as a prime objective, but those who like multi-statement lines could certainly condense the program into a much smaller number of lines.

The first part of the program consists of the MENU, which has been discussed at length earlier in this book. A useful addition might be a line such as

90 ON ERROR GOTO 120

This would return execution to the MENU whenever a mistake or the ESCAPE key were pressed.

Creating the file

The program, as usual, consists of a set of procedures driven from a menu. The first procedure, PROCcreate, requires a new filename to be INPUT, then records are INPUT in

MENU

1 Create a file
2 Read a file
3 Display a file
4 Update a file

CREATING A FILE

Records entered and written to tape/disk

READING A FILE

Records read from tape/disk to memory, and assigned to variable names

DISPLAY A FILE

Printing each record on the screen

Additional modules may be added to search, sort or print hard copy, as described previously

UPDATE A FILE

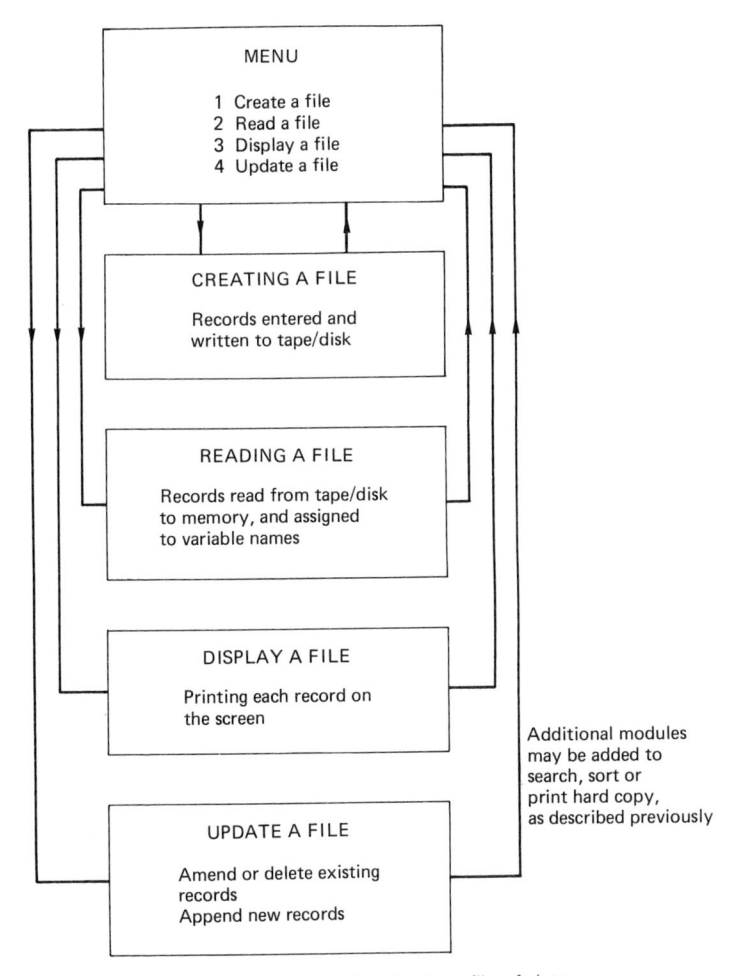

Amend or delete existing records
Append new records

Fig. 9.6 A program to create and maintain a file of data

```
100   DIM item$(100),price(100),stock%(100)
110
120   REPEAT
130      PROCmenu
140      IF option=1 THEN PROCcreate
150      IF option=2 THEN PROCread
160      IF option=3 THEN PROCdisplay
170      IF option=4 THEN PROCupdate
180      UNTIL option=5
190   END
200
210   DEF PROCmenu
220   CLS
230   PRINT TAB(8,8);"1:Create a File"
240   PRINT TAB(8,10);"2:Read a File"
```

Fig. 9.7 A program to create, display and update a sequential data file (reading from file into arrays in the memory)

```
250   PRINT TAB(8,12);"3:Display a File"
260   PRINT TAB(8,14);"4:Update a File"
270   PRINT TAB(8,16);"5:End"
280   option=GET-48
290   ENDPROC
300
310   DEF PROCcreate:CLS
320    INPUT"ENTER FILENAME "F$
330   X=OPENOUT F$
340   REPEAT
350     CLS
360      INPUT"ENTER DESCRIPTION "item$
370     IF item$="***" THEN 450
380      INPUT"ENTER PRICE "price
390      INPUT"ENTER STOCK "stock%
400     PRINT'''';"Enter R to Record"
410     PRINT"or T to Type again"
420     G$=GET$:IF G$<>"R"ANDG$<>"T"THEN420
430     IF G$="T" THEN 360
440     PRINT#X,item$,price,stock%
450     UNTIL item$="***"
460   CLOSE#X
470   ENDPROC
480
490   DEF PROCread:CLS:I=0
500    INPUT"ENTER FILENAME "F$
510   Y=OPENIN F$
520   REPEAT:I=I+1
530     INPUT#Y,item$(I),price(I),stock%(I)
540     CLS:PRINT item$(I)
550     PRINT price(I)
560     PRINT stock%(I)
570     PROCspace
580     UNTIL EOF#Y
590   CLOSE#Y
600   N=I
610   ENDPROC
620
630   DEF PROCdisplay
640   FOR I=1 TO N
650     CLS
660     PRINT"RECORD NO."I
670     PRINTitem$(I)
680     PRINT price(I)
690     PRINT stock%(I)
700     PROCspace
710     NEXT
720   ENDPROC
730
740   DEF PROCupdate
750   REPEAT:CLS
760     PRINT"ENTER THE NO. OF THE RECORD"
770     PRINT"TO BE CHANGED OR APPENDED"
780     INPUT A:IF A>N THEN N=A
790      INPUT"ENTER DESCRIPTION "item$(A)
800     IF item$(A)="***" THEN 830
```

Fig. 9.7 (continued)

Developing a complete program 87

```
810       INPUT"ENTER PRICE "price(A)
820       INPUT"ENTER STOCK "stock%(A)
830       UNTIL item$(A)="***"
840   REM Writing the New File
850   CLS
860     INPUT"ENTER FILENAME "Q$
870   Z=OPENOUT Q$
880     FOR I=1 TO N-1
890       IF item$(I)="DELETED"THEN 910
900         PRINT#Z,item$(I),price(I),stock%(I)
910     NEXT I
920   CLOSE#Z
930   ENDPROC
940
950   DEF PROCspace
960   PRINT''''"PRESS SPACE TO CONTINUE"
970   REPEAT UNTIL GET=32
980     ENDPROC
```

Fig. 9.7 (continued)

a REPEAT ... UNTIL loop. The opportunity is given to retype a record if it is not satisfactory (lines 410–430) before recording using PRINT# in line 440. (This will not cause disc activity until the buffer is full.)

To stop entering records, we test for a 'dummy' entered in *item$*. The user types "***" in response to "ENTER DESCRIPTION" when all of the DATA has been entered. The REPEAT ... UNTIL loop is then satisfied, the file is CLOSED and the DATA is written to the file.

Reading an existing file

Reading a file, in DEF PROCread, requires the name of a previously recorded file to be entered in response to "ENTER FILENAME". All of the records are read from disc or tape and displayed on the screen, under the control of the familiar PROCspace. (Note here that PROCmenu and PROCspace have been taken directly from previous programs.)

The reading of the file is terminated by the detection of the EOF#Y (line 580), and the file is CLOSED. Store N is set to I, the subscript of the last record read into the file.

Displaying a file which has been previously read

DEF PROCdisplay introduces no new ideas, but note that this can only be used after reading in an existing file during DEF PROCread.

Updating the file

DEF PROCupdate is probably the most complex of the procedures. After having read and displayed an existing file, we should have noted the numbers of any records to be altered. The record number is entered in response to the prompts at lines 760 and 770 and the amended (or appended) record is entered. Further records may be amended until this process is terminated, when the users enters the 'dummy' description "***" into store *item$(A)*, line 790. (Before entering this dummy it is necessary also to enter a dummy record number—the next available in the file.)

During this procedure records may be appended by allocating to them a record number following on from the last number in the existing file.

If a record is to be deleted it is typed with the description "DELETED" and a dummy price and stock. When the amended file is written the test at line 890 ensures that the DELETED records are not written to the new file.

Before writing the amended file, the user is asked to enter a filename at line 860. In order to preserve a copy of the original file, it is advisable to enter a new name at this stage for the amended file.

Finally, the new file, complete with amendments, is written in a FOR ... NEXT loop at lines 880–910 and the file is CLOSED.

Checking of the amended file should now be carried out using the Read and Display options.

Any unwanted obsolete data files may be deleted during *DELETE in exactly the same way as program files may be deleted. Obviously for security purposes, a backup copy of the disk should be made using *ENABLE and *BACKUP as described earlier in this chapter.

We can summarise the features of this program as follows:

- It is menu-driven
- It allows any number of data files to be created, separate from the program
- Records may be read back from disk and displayed.
- Records may be modified, deleted or appended and a new file automatically created on the disk.

The disadvantage of this method is that all of the above is accomplished by reading the DATA from the disk into array stores in the computer's memory. This imposes the limitation of the available memory size on the size of the file which may be handled.

The next section shows how this problem may be overcome to enable files, much bigger than the computer's memory, to be handled.

Handling a very large file

This method can be used when the file exceeds the available memory in the computer. No arrays will be needed, since records will be handled one at a time and overwritten in the memory by the next one read from disk.

The essential difference is that we will use the disk system's ability to handle two files simultaneously. The first, the **source** file will be opened to read. Records will be read from the source file and, if no modification is necessary will be written to the new, or **destination** file. The destination file must, of course, have been opened for writing.

We input the name of any record we wish to modify and test for this during the read operation. The name of the record would be a unique identifier entered as FIELD 1. When the required record has been found, the user is asked to enter the updated version, which is then written to disk. This process continues until the end of the source file is detected by EOF# and the source file is CLOSED.

However, before closing the destination file, the opportunity is given to add further records to the end, until the user signifies completion of the operation by entering "***" as FIELD1. The destination file will then be CLOSED and all writing to the disk will be completed. To remove an unwanted record, as before, we can simply type a dummy

FIELD1, such as "DELETED" and use this to by-pass the write operation (PRINT #
etc.). The whole process is shown diagrammatically in Fig. 9.8.

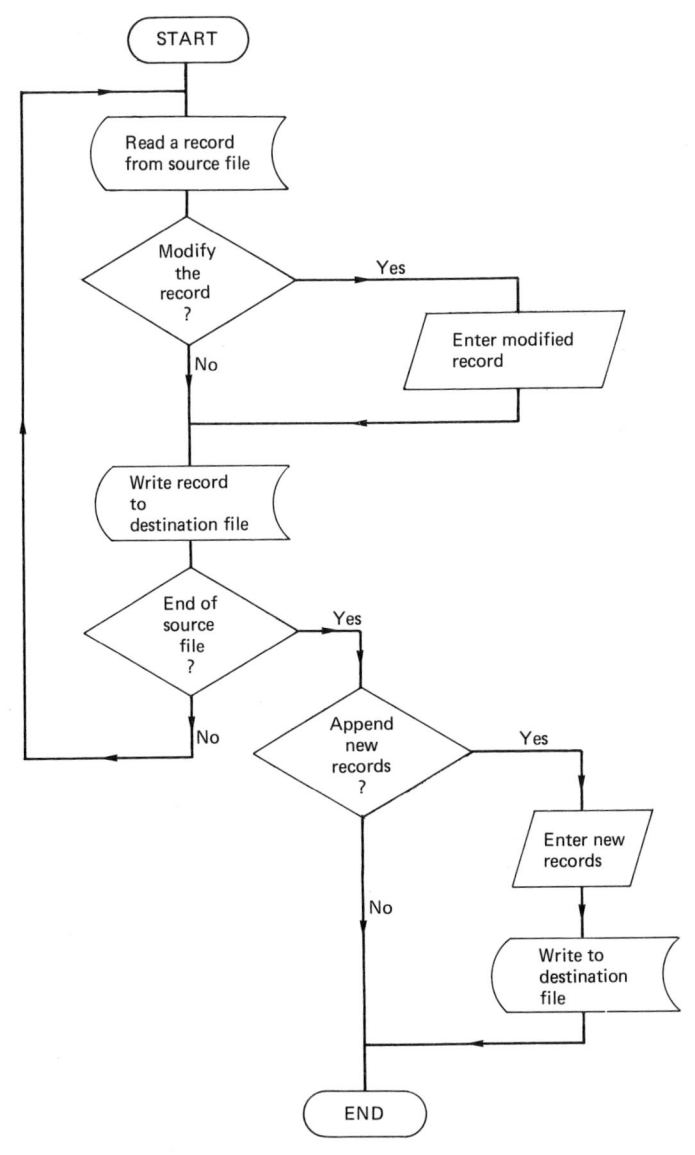

Fig. 9.8 Copying records from a source file to a destination file with options to modify, delete or append records

For demonstration purposes, we can again use the stock of the sportshop described earlier. The program will be based on the array version, Fig. 9.7 with the following modifications. We will not need any dimension statement, and the menu can be used with only slight changes.

DEF PROCcreate remains unaltered.

90 Data Files

DEF PROCread will be similar, without the need for subscript I. We will not need to separate PROCdisplay.

The main difference will be in DEF PROCupdate which must be rewritten from scratch. The variable list used in the example is the stocklist for the sportshop *item$, price, stock%* but the reader obviously may wish to enter a more extensive set of variables for another application. The complete program is shown in Fig. 9.9.

```
100    ONERROR GOTO 120
110
120    REPEAT
130      PROCmenu
140      IF option=1 THEN PROCcreate
150      IF option=2 THEN PROCread
160      IF option=3 THEN PROCupdate
170      UNTIL option=4
180    END
190
200    DEF PROCmenu
210    CLS
220    PRINT TAB(8,8);"1:Create a File"
230    PRINT TAB(8,10);"2:Read a File"
240    PRINT TAB(8,14);"3:Update a File"
250    PRINT TAB(8,16);"4:End"
260    option=GET-48
270    ENDPROC
280
290    DEF PROCcreate:CLS
300      INPUT"ENTER FILENAME "F$
310    X=OPENOUT F$
320    REPEAT
330      CLS
340        INPUT"ENTER DESCRIPTION "item$
350      IF item$="***" THEN 430
360        INPUT"ENTER PRICE "price
370        INPUT"ENTER STOCK "stock%
380      PRINT'''';"Enter R to Record"
390      PRINT"or T to Type again"
400      G$=GET$:IF G$<>"R"ANDG$<>"T"THEN400
410      IF G$="T" THEN 340
420      PRINT#X,item$,price,stock%
430      UNTIL item$="***"
440    CLOSE#X
450    ENDPROC
460
470    DEF PROCread:CLS
480      INPUT"ENTER FILENAME "F$
490    Y=OPENIN F$
500    REPEAT
510      INPUT#Y,item$,price,stock%
520      CLS:PRINT item$
530      PRINT price
540      PRINT stock%
550      PROCspace
560      UNTIL EOF#Y
```

Fig. 9.9 A program to handle files which exceed the computer's available memory

```
570   CLOSE#Y
580   ENDPROC
590
600   DEF PROCupdate:CLS
610     INPUT"NAME SOURCE FILE"S$
620     S=OPENIN S$
630     INPUT"NAME DESTINATION FILE"D$
640     D=OPENOUT D$
650   CLS:PRINT"ENTER THE NAME OF THE"
660   PRINT"RECORD TO BE MODIFIED"
670   INPUT change$
680   REPEAT
690     INPUT#S,item$,price,stock%
700     IF item$<>change$ THEN 750
710     INPUT"ENTER DESCRIPTION"item$
720      IF item$="DELETED"   THEN 760
730     INPUT"ENTER PRICE"price
740     INPUT"ENTER STOCK"stock%
750     PRINT#D,item$,price,stock%
760     UNTIL EOF#S
770   CLS
780   PRINT"APPENDING RECORDS"
790   PROCspace
800   REPEAT:CLS
810     INPUT"ENTER DESCRIPTION"item$
820     IF item$="***" THEN 860
830     INPUT"ENTER PRICE"price
840     INPUT"ENTER STOCK"stock%
850     PRINT#D,item$,price,stock%
860     UNTIL item$="***"
870   CLOSE#D
880   ENDPROC
890
900   DEF PROCspace
910   PRINT''''"PRESS SPACE TO CONTINUE"
920   REPEAT UNTIL GET=32
930   ENDPROC
```

Fig. 9.9 (continued)

Two files are OPENed simultaneously. Records are read from the source file, modified if necessary, and written to the destination file. No arrays are used, so the size of the file is limited by the available disk space, not the computer memory. We can summarise this program as follows:

- A file of any size (within the capacity of the disk) may be created.
- The file can be read and displayed on the screen.
- The file may be updated by:
  modifying a record
  deleting a record
  appending records.

We could easily add a further procedure to search for and print an individual record or set of records, but this involves no new ideas and is left as an exercise for the reader.

It is hoped that the reader will now be able to write a useful sequential file handling program to perform a realistic task on a very large set of records. Obviously the variable list must be altered throughout to cater for records of a different type.

92 Data Files

At this point it might be worth considering the planning and developing of a program, to minimise the frustration caused by unnecessary errors and duplication of previous work.

Programming strategy

While everyone has their own individual style of working, I find the following system helps when developing large programs.

1. Plan program modules on paper, well away from the computer.
2. Convert to BASIC code, 'cannibalising' any existing procedures from the listings of earlier programs.
3. Check the coding for errors.
4. Enter the program, SAVING on disc, at intervals (say every page). Do not attempt to RUN.
5. Obtain a printed listing and check for errors.
6. Correct any errors and reSAVE.
7. RUN and debug.
8. SAVE the final copy and make a duplicate on a separate disk.

Since the display of the disk catalogue (obtained by typing *.) does not distinguish between **program** files and **data** files, it may be helpful to append a code to their names when they are SAVEd or written to disk. For example, the names of all program files might be suffixed with the letter P.

The case for random access files

This section has described a method of maintaining a large sequential file. The main disadvantage with the sequential file is that the whole of the original file must be read and completely rewritten to include any modifications. Obviously this is not ideal because of the time involved and the increased risk of error in resaving the whole file. For instance, a file containing 1000 names would have to be read and rewritten in its entirety even if only one name needed amendment. This inefficiency arises because sequential filing does not keep a record of the exact positions of individual pieces of DATA stored on the disk. The DATA is recorded as a continuous string, in effect like the recordings on a cassette.

Random access files, however, employ the pointer facility (PTR#) to enable the programmer to specify the position on the disk where each piece of DATA begins. It is therefore possible to locate the exact position of a single piece of DATA, and carry out any necessary modifications, while leaving the remainder of the file unchanged.

The next chapter covers the use of the pointer to modify individual fields in a random access file.

10
Random Access Files

The ability to locate and modify an individual record is a crucial advantage of data files on disk compared with files stored on cassette. While virtually all of the preceding work in this book may also be carried out on cassette, the following pages on random access files apply only to disk-based systems.

Random access, i.e. the retrieving or writing of DATA at any point on the disk, is made possible by the PTR# command. This specifies the byte position (one byte being the space occupied by one character) where the moving head begins reading or writing. When a new file is recorded, writing starts at byte 0. The pointer may be moved to start writing the second record a prescribed number of characters from the first by a simple BASIC statement involving PTR#.

The essential features of the random access file are therefore:

- The data is written to the file in a similar way to the sequential file.
- The pointer specifies a number at which each record (or individual field) begins.
- A particular record can be accessed for reading or modifying without reference to previous records in the file.

Now although we can proceed directly to a desired record, this does imply that we already know either:

1 the pointer value at which the record begins, or
2 a method of calculating the pointer position.

The second condition requires the pointer position to be calculated by the use of fixed record lengths, by the formula

  pointer value = (No. of records − 1) × No. of characters per record

The situation is further complicated by the fact that the data can consist of either integers, floating point variables or strings. When these three types of DATA are written to a file they occupy different numbers of bytes, as summarised in the following table.

Type of DATA	No. of bytes per field
Integer	5
Floating point	6
String	No. of characters in the string + 2

94 Random Access Files

In order to clarify this rather confused picture we will write a simple file creation program containing each type of data, integer, floating point and string. We will then read the file back, displaying the pointer value throughout the file.

For the purposes of this simple demonstration, the DATA will be entered via READ and DATA statements, not INPUT statements which would be more suitable for practical programs. To demonstrate the use of string, integer and floating point DATA as simply as possible, we will consider a set of 3 world speed records.

FIELD 1	FIELD 2	FIELD 3
TYPE	SPEED(MPH)	YEAR
LAND	739.666	1979
WATER	319.627	1978
MOTOR CYCLE	313.66	1978

We will use meaningful variable names as follows:

type$: string store for type of speed record
speed: floating point store for the speed attained
year%: integer variable for the year of the record

The program to create and read this very small file is shown in Fig. 10.1.

```
10    REM writing the file
20    X=OPENOUT"FASTEST"
30    FOR N=1 TO 3
40      READtype$,speed,year%
50      PRINT#X,type$,speed,year%
60    NEXT
70    CLOSE#X
80    REM reading the file
90    CLS
100   Y=OPENIN"FASTEST"
110   REPEAT
120     PRINT"POINTER "PTR#Y;
130     INPUT#Y,type$:PRINTtype$
140     PRINT"POINTER "PTR#Y;
150     INPUT#Y,speed:PRINTspeed
160     PRINT"POINTER "PTR#Y;
170     INPUT#Y,year%:PRINTyear%
180   UNTIL EOF#Y
190   PRINT"LENGTH OF FILE "EXT#Y
200   CLOSE#Y
210   DATA LAND,739.666,1979
220   DATA WATER,319.627,1978
230   DATA MOTOR CYCLE,318.66,1978
```

Fig. 10.1 A simple 3 record program to demonstrate the use of the PTR# command to give the pointer position at the start of each field in a record.

This demonstration program (Fig.10.1) reads the DATA and writes it to disk in a sequential file during lines 20–70.

Reading the pointer value

After opening for a read operation, line 120 prints the value of the pointer, using PTR#Y. This is the initial value of the pointer, prior to reading the first field of the first record in the file. This is achieved at line 130, where the INPUT#Y statement reads the type from disk into memory, into store *type$*. This variable is then printed on the screen.

Detecting the end of file EOF#

This process continues until the whole file has been read and printed, together with the corresponding pointer positions. The REPEAT ... UNTIL loop is terminated at line 180 by the detection of the end of the file, using EOF#Y.

Length of the file EXT#

Line 190 displays the total number of bytes or characters in the file using the extent command EXT#Y. Note the use of the channel, in this case Y, which must be included consistently throughout the opening of the file in all file commands such as PRINT#Y, INPUT#Y, PTR#Y, EOF#Y, EXT#Y and CLOSE#Y.

The results of running this program are shown in Fig. 10.2. The first piece of data, the word LAND is written at position 0. Since this is a string it occupies its own length plus two additional bytes. The second field, 739.666 is written starting at byte position 6. All floating point numbers occupy 6 bytes, so 739.666 occupies byte positions 6 to 11 inclusive. Thus the next field, the year 1979, is started at position 12 and being an integer variable occupies 5 bytes, i.e. 12–16 inclusive. The next field WATER therefore begins at position 17.

We may check the length of the file (59 bytes), obtained by the use of EXT#, in various ways. For instance, the last field, the year 1978, is written at byte position 54 and since it is an integer variable, occupies a further 5 bytes to the end of the file.

Pointer position	Data
0	LAND
6	739.666
12	1979
17	WATER
24	319.627
30	1978
35	MOTOR CYCLE
48	318.66
54	1978

LENGTH OF FILE 59 (BYTES)

Fig. 10.2

Using BGET# to examine the file a byte at a time

The BGET# command enables a single byte to be read from the disk. The following short program will enable us to read back the 59 characters of the file "FASTEST", giving a detailed picture of the way the three types of DATA, i.e. string, floating point and integer, are recorded on disk.

```
100 Y=OPENIN"FASTEST"
110 REPEAT
120    PRINT BGET#Y;
130    UNTIL EOF#Y
140 CLOSE#Y
```

When this program is run, the output is as follows:

0	4	68	78	65	76	255	190
159	234	56	138	65	0	0	7
187	0	5	82	69	84	65	87
255	137	65	208	31	137	64	0
0	7	186	0	11	69	76	67
89	67	32	82	79	84	79	77
255	225	122	84	31	137	64	0
0	7	186					

Fig. 10.3 Reading a file a byte at a time, using BGET#

The above apparently meaningless list of numbers is actually the set of 59 bytes which form our file of world records. Each byte has been displayed as the ASCII code of its contents. It is therefore easy to pick out the letters, so the 3rd, 4th, 5th and 6th bytes represent DNAL, the first field in the file, i.e. the word LAND (strings are written to a file backwards).

The 4 which precedes this is the number of characters in the string LAND.

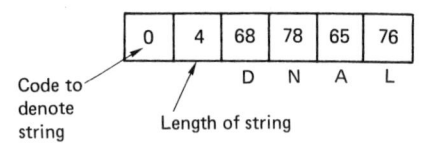

0	4	68	78	65	76
		D	N	A	L

Code to denote string ← ↑ Length of string

The same pattern is repeated for the other two strings in the file.

0	5	82	69	84	65	87
		R	E	T	A	W

0	11	69	76	67	89	67	32	82	79	84	79	77
		E	L	C	Y	C		R	O	T	O	M

(32 above is the ASCII code for a space.)

Modifying a single field on the disk, using OPENUP

The 0 at the front of each string is a code to denote that what follows is string rather than numerical data. This is commonly represented as the hexadecimal byte &00.

Following this pattern we see that the next set of bytes begins with 255 and there are 2 further sets of 6 bytes beginning with 255. These are the floating point numbers representing the speeds for each of the world records. 255 is actually the denary representation of the hexadecimal number &FF, which is used to denote that a floating point number follows.

Finally we can see (in Fig. 10.3), three sets of 5 byte numbers, each beginning with 64. These are the years, each stored as integer variables in 5 bytes. The 64 is the denary equivalent of the hexadecimal code &40, used to denote integer variables. The storage of data on disk can therefore be summarised as follows:

Type of Data	First Byte	Remaining Bytes
String	&00	1 byte for length of string plus string itself
Floating point	&FF	5 bytes containing the number
Integer	&40	4 bytes containing the integer

Modifying a single field on the disk, using OPENUP

Numerical fields

Knowing the byte position at which a field starts enables us to modify that single field while leaving the remainder of the file unaltered.

Referring to Fig. 10.2, supposing we wished to modify the water speed record from 319.627 to 325.932 mph. This field begins at pointer position 24, so we open the file to write and replace the old speed by an instruction to write at position 24. We will achieve this using the program shown in Fig. 10.4.

```
 10   REM modifying a file
 20   Z=OPENUP "FASTEST"
 30   PTR#Z=24
 40   speed = 325.932
 50   PRINT#Z,speed
 60   CLOSE#Z
 70   CLS
 80   REM reading the modified file
 90   Q=OPENIN"FASTEST"
100   REPEAT
110      INPUT#Q,type$,speed,year%
120      PRINT type$,speed,year%
130   UNTIL EOF#Q
140   CLOSE#Q
```

Fig. 10.4 A simple demonstration program to modify a single field, using OPENUP and PTR#

Note that when modifying an existing file we must open the file using OPENUP—which allows both reading and writing. The use of OPENOUT would delete the whole of the original file.

As mentioned previously, all numerical data occupies a fixed number of bytes on the disk—5 for integer numbers and 6 for floating point. So there is no problem with the above example when we are replacing one floating point number with another, since both will occupy 6 bytes.

Modifying strings

Strings present a problem since they are recorded literally; the first byte denotes string data, the second gives the number of characters in the string, then the complete string follows. There is no problem if we overwrite a file with a string which is equal in length or shorter than the original string. If, however, we replace an existing string by a longer one, the latter may impinge on the next string recorded. This problem must be overcome by the use of fixed length fields and by accurate use of the pointer when writing and modifying fields.

Fixed length fields

Where it is necessary to modify string data periodically, it is therefore essential to have fields of a fixed number of characters.

If data was prepared for entry by writing it out on a standard form it would be possible to ensure that all strings had the same length, either by abbreviation, or by filling up using some arbitrary symbol, such as ***. Typing errors on entry, however, would cause problems. The next chapter discusses the creation of fixed length fields by truncation and padding: this is a rather complicated procedure but overcomes the problems discussed so far.

We can ensure that each field is written at the correct position by a statement such as

```
10000 PTR#X = PTR#X + 30
```

Before attempting to write a complete program to maintain a random access file, let us summarise the work covered so far:

- The pointer specifies a number at which reading or writing may begin.
- We can modify an individual field by specifying the pointer number, after opening the file with a suitable OPENUP statement.
- Real numbers (stored as floating point variables) and integers may easily be replaced with new numbers of the same type. This is because the representation of each type of number always occupies the same number of bytes on the disk, regardless of the number of digits in the number itself.
- A string cannot always be replaced by a new string of different length—fixed length fields should be created, either at the DATA preparation stage or by programming.
- The advantage to be gained by accessing a record randomly is obtained at the expense of more complex programming (the need to calculate pointer position, create fixed length records).

Note: when testing file programs, it is inevitable that errors will occur before all of the required CLOSE # statements have been executed. When this happens subsequent running of the program will produce 'file open' error messages. The statement CLOSE #0 typed in immediate mode will close any files left open in this way. Alternatively this may be achieved by programming the CLOSE #0 statement via an ON ERROR GOTO ... statement.

Modifying a single field on the disk, using OPENUP 99

So far this chapter has used simple demonstration programs to describe the use of the pointer to access files randomly. To be of any practical use for large files we would need to enter the DATA via INPUT statements. Similarly, we would need a menu to allow various options such as

- Create a file
- Read a record
- Modify a record
- Append a record

(further options may be programmed as PROCEDURES as described earlier in this book).

As an example, let us consider a file consisting of 5 string fields. Numeric fields could be included quite easily by altering the variable list, if calculation were necessary. Alternatively, numeric data could be INPUT as strings and converted to numbers by VAL.

Such a file might be used for names and addresses. To make the file suitable for general use rather than a particular application, we will label the fields *field1$* to *field5$* inclusive. Now in order to gain random access to the records we must have two pieces of information.

1 The number of the record within the file.
2 The number of characters in each record.

For this example, we will access a record, rather than an individual field within the record. The latter could be quite easily achieved by the same method, however, provided the number of bytes in each field were known. This approach seems reasonable, since if we wish to update a mailing list, it is likely that the entire address will have changed—not just the street or post code.

The number of the record within the file should be known from the original data. Alternatively, a simple file could be created from our main file. This would involve reading all of the names into a new sequential file, then recording, together with an appropriate record number. This index file would then be opened and read sequentially whenever the record number of a certain person or name needed to be found. This would be quicker than reading the entire main file sequentially to find the required name. The techniques necessary to produce the index file have been covered earlier in this book, and the next program is written on the assumption that the record number is known.

We must now decide on the lengths of the five fields in our record. A possible format for names and addresses is shown in this example:

Name of Field	Sample Data	Maximum Characters
FIELD1	WILLIAMSON MICHAEL JOHN	30
FIELD2	30 CHESTNUT GROVE	20
FIELD3	HATTON	10
FIELD4	NEWSHIRE	10
FIELD5	DB7 5DN	10
	TOTAL BYTES PER RECORD	80

(Remember, the actual maxima will be 2 characters less than the figures shown.)

So the pointer position for record number 95, for example, would be obtained by the

100 Random Access Files

formula

$$\text{Pointer} = (\text{Record No.} - 1) \times \text{Record Length}$$
$$= 94 \times 80$$
$$= 7520$$

This is the position at which the pointer must be set, to begin writing the modified record. It could be programmed in the following way:

```
660  DEF PROCupdate:CLS
670    INPUT'''"ENTER FILENAME "F$
680    Z=OPENUP F$
690    INPUT'''"ENTER RECORD NO. "record
700    PTR#Z=(record-1)*80
710    P=PTR#Z:CLS
720    INPUT'''"ENTER FIELD 1 "field1$
725    PRINT#Z,field1$:PTR#Z=P+30
730  INPUT"ENTER FIELD 2 "field2$
735    PRINT#Z,field2$:PTR#Z=P+50
740  INPUT"ENTER FIELD 3 "field3$
745    PRINT#Z,field3$:PTR#Z=P+60
750  INPUT"ENTER FIELD 4 "field4$
755    PRINT#Z,field4$:PTR#Z=P+70
760  INPUT"ENTER FIELD 5 "field5$
765    PRINT#Z,field5$:PTR#Z=P+80
820  CLOSE#Z:ENDPROC
```

Fig. 10.5 Modifying an individual record using OPENUP and the pointer PTR#

In the section of a program given in Fig. 10.5, F$ represents the name of a file to be modified, which may be one of several similar files on the same disk. After calculating the pointer position in the manner described above, the pointer is advanced along the file to this position. *field1$* of the new record is written, overwriting the first field of the previous record. The pointer is then positioned in the correct place to begin writing *field2$* of the modified record. When all of the five fields have been entered, the file is closed and the user is returned to the menu. The complete program is given in Fig. 10.6.

```
100    ON ERROR GOTO 120
110
120    REPEAT
130      PROCmenu
140      IF option=1 THEN PROCcreate
150      IF option=2 THEN PROCread
160      IF option=3 THEN PROCupdate
170      UNTIL option=4
180    END
190
200    DEF PROCmenu
210    CLS
220    PRINT TAB(8,8);"1:Create a File"
230    PRINT TAB(8,10);"2:Read a File"
240     PRINT TAB(8,12);"3:Update a File"
250     PRINT TAB(8,14);"4:End"
260    option=GET-48
270    ENDPROC
280
```

Fig. 10.6 A menu-driven program to create, read and maintain a random access file

Modifying a single field on the disk, using OPENUP

```
290   DEF PROCcreate:CLS
300     INPUT'''"ENTER FILENAME "F$
310   X=OPENOUT F$
320   A=0
330   REPEAT
340      INPUT'''"ENTER FIELD 1 "field1$
350     IF field1$="***" THEN 450
360     PRINT#X,field1$:PTR#X=A+30
370     INPUT"ENTER FIELD 2 "field2$
380     PRINT#X,field2$:PTR#X=A+50
390     INPUT"ENTER FIELD 3 "field3$
400     PRINT#X,field3$:PTR#X=A+60
410     INPUT"ENTER FIELD 4 "field4$
420     PRINT#X,field4$:PTR#X=A+70
430     INPUT"ENTER FIELD 5 "field5$
440     PRINT#X,field5$:PTR#X=A+80
444     A=A+80
445     PRINTPTR#X
450     UNTIL field1$="***"
460   CLOSE#X:ENDPROC
470
480   DEF PROCread:CLS
490     INPUT'''"ENTER FILENAME "F$
500   Y=OPENUP F$
510     INPUT'''"ENTER RECORD NO. "record
520    PTR#Y=(record-1)*80
530   P=PTR#Y
540   INPUT#Y,field1$:PTR#Y=P+30
550   INPUT#Y,field2$:PTR#Y=P+50
560   INPUT#Y,field3$:PTR#Y=P+60
570   INPUT#Y,field4$:PTR#Y=P+70
580   INPUT#Y,field5$:PTR#Y=P+80
590   CLS:PRINT'''';field1$
600   PRINT'';field2$:PRINT'';field3$
610   PRINT'';field4$:PRINT'';field5$
620    PRINT''';"Press Space To Continue"
630    REPEAT UNTIL GET=32
640   CLOSE#Y:ENDPROC
650
660    DEF PROCupdate:CLS
670     INPUT'''"ENTER FILENAME "F$
680    Z=OPENUP F$
690     INPUT'''"ENTER RECORD NO. "record
700    PTR#Z=(record-1)*80
710    P=PTR#Z:CLS
720     INPUT'''"ENTER FIELD 1 "field1$
725    PRINT#Z,field1$:PTR#Z=P+30
730   INPUT"ENTER FIELD 2 "field2$
735    PRINT#Z,field2$:PTR#Z=P+50
740   INPUT"ENTER FIELD 3 "field3$
745    PRINT#Z,field3$:PTR#Z=P+60
750   INPUT"ENTER FIELD 4 "field4$
755    PRINT#Z,field4$:PTR#Z=P+70
760   INPUT"ENTER FIELD 5 "field5$
765    PRINT#Z,field5$:PTR#Z=P+80
820   CLOSE#Z:ENDPROC
```

Fig. 10.6 (continued)

Creating the file—moving the pointer

Referring to the complete program, (Fig. 10.6), the menu is a direct copy from an earlier program in this book. In DEF PROCcreate the file is opened to write, after being given a suitable short name, such as "MAIL". We then enter the five fields of the first record in response to INPUT prompts and we continue entering records in a REPEAT ... UNTIL loop. When all of the records of the file have been entered we terminate the loop by entering "***", to signify the end of the data. This is tested for at line 450 to prevent the dummy record being written to disk.

Note that after writing each field to disk, the pointer is advanced by the required number of bytes ready for the entry of the next field. For example, we have allocated 30 bytes for *field1$*, so after writing *field1$* we have the statement

```
PTR#X = A + 30
```

(A is simply an arbitrary counter which was initially set to 0 and is advanced by 80 at the end of each record.) In the same way the remaining fields are entered and written to disk before the pointer is advanced by the specified number of bytes.

When the loop is terminated (by the user entering "***") the file is closed.

Reading a single record—calculation of pointer position

During DEF PROCread, the required file is opened using OPENUP. We then enter the number of the record to be read and from this the pointer position is calculated using

```
520 PTR#Y = (record-1)*80
```

Since, in this example, there are 80 characters per record, this gives the pointer position at the *beginning* of the required record. The record is displayed and the user is returned to the menu via depression of the space bar.

Modifying a single record

The required file is again opened for modification using OPENUP, and the required record number is entered. This enables the pointer position to be calculated to give the start of the required record.

The user is then instructed to enter the new version of the record and this single record overwrites the previous record in this position. Provided we do not exceed the field length which we originally allocated, the new record will replace the old quite correctly. Bearing in mind, however, that the first two bytes are used to describe the string, if we exceed the prescribed field length we will have problems with the next field to be recorded. A simple example will illustrate this more clearly.

Supposing we have part of a file as follows:

0	5	N	W	O	R	B	0	5	H	T	I	M	S

We might try to overwrite BROWN with WILLIAMS. If we had programmed a pointer movement of 7 bytes to the beginning of the next field, a problem will occur. The next field will overlap the name Williams, which (having been written backwards), will be truncated to SMAIL.

A string such as "JONES" may be replaced with a shorter string, such as "FOX", without any difficulty.

Appending a record

Adding records to the end of the file is carried out very easily during DEF PROCupdate. It is simply a case of entering the record number which immediately succeeds the last record in the existing file. So if we have 100 records in a file which we wish to extend, then we enter 101 as the number of the record to be appended. From this the correct pointer position is calculated and the new record is appended to the file. The CLOSE # statement writes a new EOF # to mark the end of the extended file.

Deleting a record

Since we do not ever re-record the whole file, we cannot delete the space occupied by a record in a random file, in the way that it may be omitted when a sequential file is rewritten. If, in the case of a mailing list, it was necessary to delete a name from a circulation, it would be advisable to:

overwrite the record with obviously 'dummy' data, *or*
overwrite the record with a new, valid record.

Summary

The program, Fig. 10.6, represents a framework on which a larger, more versatile program may be built. This might be achieved by the following additions:

- Further procedures, such as sorting or searching.
- Improve layout and user-friendly instructions.
- Increased variable list.
- Programming to check that fixed length fields are not exceeded.

The above refinements were not included, as the required techniques are covered earlier in this book and would only have 'clouded' the essential new features of random access.

Such a program might be used wherever it is necessary to alter individual records periodically. Typical applications might be the employee list of a small company or similar organisation, or the membership of a club.

Note that it is possible to have a large number of files on one disk, and access them from the same program. It is advisable, however, to start a large and important file on a new disk. This is because all new files are allocated 64 sectors when they are created— a total of 16K bytes. If the file is likely to need more than this amount of disk space, then the required amount should be reserved by creating a large dummy file. This can be done by using a FOR ... NEXT loop to write the same dummy record to disk a given number of times. Any future files will be opened beyond the dummy data on the disk. The latter may then be overwritten as the real data file is written.

The next chapter continues this work with an attempt to produce a general purpose data base program. New features included are:

1   The creation of fixed length fields by truncation or padding.
2   The reservation of disk space for extending data files.

11

Towards a Viable Data Base Program

Introduction

The previous chapters gave skeleton programs which are intended to demonstrate the basic techniques needed to process data. In this chapter we will produce a general-purpose program which should enable an unskilled operator to carry out useful work. This will basically consist of entering data in response to simple instructions. I have used this program with students from a variety of backgrounds wishing to create and maintain files on a wide range of subjects such as:

- Records of farmers as customers of an agricultural merchant
- Membership details of caravan clubs and vintage car clubs
- Car and aircraft performance details
- Classification of a personal music collection
- Surgical instruments and nursing equipment required in the operating theatre for various operations

In order to maintain the frequently changing details of these files, the program must include, amongst other things, the following options:

- To search for a single record, with random access
- To locate and modify a single field within a record
- To add records continually to the end of the file

The ability to overwrite existing data on the disk ad infinitum is one of the greatest virtues of the magnetic disk, and the precision which enables us to change just a single character really distinguishes the disk from a cassette-based system. One of the largest manufacturers of floppy disks claims that every piece of data can be changed every hour of every day for 200 years.

Since the files are held on disk and records are only held singly in the computer's memory, the limitation to file size is simply the free capacity on the disk—not the available RAM in the computer. Using a new disk for a file we might, therefore, use a 100K system to hold approximately 500 records if each record contained 200 characters. For larger files the user would need to consider the purchase of an 80 track drive or a Winchester hard disk system.

Methods of determining the available disk space and therefore the number of records which can be accommodated will be discussed in detail later in this chapter.

The record format

The sample application used to demonstrate the program will be a Staff Personnel File. Each record will consist of 10 fields. The program is suitable for any application—it is simply a case of designing the required record consisting of field names and field lengths. For simplicity these are held in data statements, while a more user-friendly method would create a small file.

It is necessary at the outset to design the record format, i.e. the field names and the field lengths. It must be borne in mind that in MODE 7, only 40 characters can be accommodated across the screen including the field name e.g.

```
0                                          39
0.NAME:JOHNSON MICHAEL W.
1.ADDRESS:152 WINDMILL LANE
```

The use of MODE 0 with 80 characters per line will permit greater field lengths, but will require a high quality monitor for legibility.

The record format for the personnel file is shown in Table 11.1.

Table 11.1 A record from the personnel file

No.	Field Name	Sample Data	Fixed Field Length	Length on Disk
0	NAME	JOHNSON MICHAEL W.	30	32
1	ADDRESS	152 WINDMILL LANE	28	30
2	D. OF B.	30.11.49	8	10
3	DESCRIPTION	DESIGNER	10	12
4	QUALIFICATIONS	B.Sc.	9	11
5	NAT.INS.NO.	YL654328E	9	11
6	DATE JOINED	09.03.75	8	10
7	SALARY	£12,000	6	8
8	PREVIOUS EMPLOY.	UNITED PRODUCTS	20	22
9	DATE LEFT	N/A	8	10
		TOTAL	136	156

Note that when each field is written to disk a further 2 characters or bytes are added. The first is a single byte (0) to denote that string data follows, while the second byte contains the number of characters in the string.

So our personnel file has 10 fields and a total of 156 characters per record. When the file is created, the operator will enter data in response to INPUT prompts. Any field which is above the specified field length will be truncated using LEFT$. A field which is below the required length will be padded with dummy bytes (spaces) to the fixed field length.

After all 10 fields have been entered by the operator, the complete record will be displayed on the screen in its truncated/padded form. An important feature of the program is that the opportunity is given to retype one or more fields. This is particularly helpful if the field has been truncated in an unsatisfactory fashion and a more satisfactory abbreviation can be entered. Alternatively it provides an opportunity to correct a copying error before the record is written to disk.

The process is summarised in Fig. 11.1.

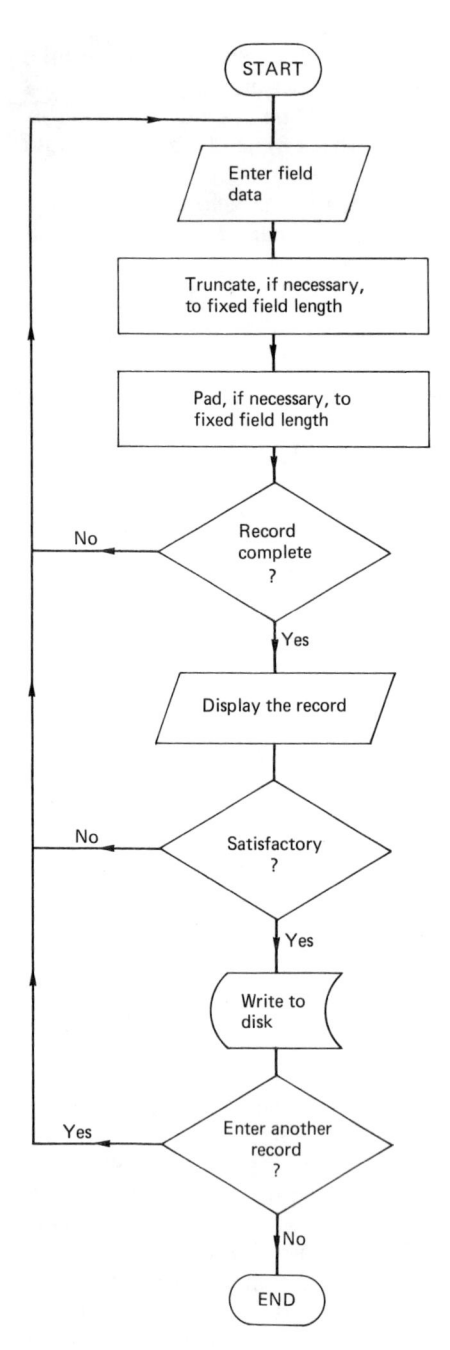

Fig. 11.1 The process of entering, truncating, padding and checking fields before the record is written to disk.

Fixing the field length

Now the program must be able to handle fields which are less than, equal to, and greater than the fixed field length. We will therefore carry out a test to check the contents of the stores at each stage. Using a few lines of BASIC code and assuming for convenience a fixed length field of 10 characters, we can test words of various lengths.

```
10 INPUT name$
20 name$=LEFT$(name$,10)←─────────────────────────Truncating
30 name$=name$+STRING$((10-LEN(name$)),CHR$32)←───Padding
40 PRINT name$,"LENGTH"LEN(name$)
```

Fig. 11.2 An example to show the creation of a fixed field length of 10 characters

When this program is run using the words BROWN, WILLIAMSON and CONSTANTINOPLE, the results shown in Table 11.2 are obtained.

Table. 11.2 The effect on names of various lengths when converted to a fixed field length of 10 characters

NAME	BROWN	WILLIAMSON	CONSTANTINOPLE
NO. OF CHARACTERS	5	10	14
NAME AFTER TRUNCATION USING LEFT$	BROWN	WILLIAMSON	CONSTANTIN
NO. OF CHARACTERS	5	10	10
NAME AFTER TRUNCATION AND PADDING.	BROWN	WILLIAMSON	CONSTANTIN
NO. OF CHARACTERS	10	10	10

The statement STRING$(10,"*") for example, supplies 10 asterisks. Similarly, the statement STRING$((10-LEN(name$),CHR$32) supplies a certain number of CHR$32, i.e. spaces. The number of spaces is 10-LEN(name$) i.e. the number of spaces required to pad the name upto 10 characters.

It can be seen that although BROWN only needs padding, the action of truncation using LEFT$ causes no problem. Similarly, CONSTANTINOPLE requires no padding but the truncated result CONSTANTIN might be unacceptable and a more suitable abbreviation might need to be entered.

Note that the truncation operation must be carried out before the padding. This is because if the original field exceeds the fixed field length, STRING$((10-LEN(name$)), CHR$32) will produce a negative quantity in 10-LEN(name$). Truncating to 10 characters before attempting to pad ensures that this cannot happen.

CHR$32 in line 30 (Fig. 11.2) is the code for a space—the character used in padding.

So we create a file having every record identical in format. In my example, all records will occupy 156 characters on the disk. All fields in one record will have the same number of characters as the corresponding fields in every other record. This homogeneity throughout the file allows the position of every record and every field to be calculated and accessed with precision via the pointer.

108 *Towards a Viable Data Base Program*

File size

After entering all of the records in the file, the file could be closed. However, if it is subsequently necessary to extend the file a problem may occur.

When a file is to be created, the disk filing system (DFS) looks for a space 64 sectors in length—a total of 64 × 256 bytes or 16K. After completion the file is closed down to its actual size. Now should a later file be written to disk it may well impinge on the space required to expand the first file. It is therefore necessary to extend the new file beyond the size of its genuine data in order to reserve space for future expansion. In the same way a company might buy adjoining land to provide for future expansion of its facilities.

The data file is easily extended at the creation stage by writing a set of dummy records which are appended to the genuine records. When the file is extended, each new genuine record exactly overwrites each dummy record. Further, when reading the file, the first dummy record can be used as a marker to detect the end of the file of actual data.

A simple routine to write 20 dummy records to a file would be

```
540 FOR T=1 TO 20:FOR N=0 TO 9
550 PRINT#X,STRING$(length(N),"*")
560 NEXT N:NEXT T
```

N is the number of the field, *length(N)* is the field length. A set of 20 complete dummy records is written to disk, each field being identical in length to the genuine fields. Of course, for an important file, the cost of dedicating a new disk to this one file should not be prohibitive and will reduce the likelihood of a 'can't extend' error.

If an existing disk must be used then two steps can be taken to maximise the space available for the new file:

1 Delete any unwanted files or programs, (using *DELETE⟨filename⟩).
2 Amalgamate all spaces scattered throughout the disk into a single usable area, using *COMPACT

How many records per disk?

Assuming your disk is not new, *COMPACT will create the maximum usable space on the disk and inform you of the number of characters available. The procedure for calculating the number of records which will fit on the disk can best be demonstrated by an example.

After compacting using *COMP., a 100K disk produced the following display:

```
*COMPACT

$.FIX L FF1B00 FF8023 000AA4 002

Disk compacted 183 free sectors
```

183 in this case is a hexadecimal number, so that instead of hundreds, tens, and units, its place values are

256s	16s	1s
1	8	3

Converting 183 to decimal, we have (1 × 256) + (8 × 16) + (3 × 1) i.e. 387 free sectors.

Now since each sector contains 256 characters, the amount of space available on the disk is 387 × 256 = 99072 characters. Working with a record length of 156 characters, the number of records which this disk can accommodate is

98072 ÷ 156 = 635.077

To verify these figures, I created a dummy file called "TEST" consisting of 635 records, as described earlier, and then compacted the disk again.

The screen display was as follows:

```
*COMPACT

$.FIX  L  FF1800  FF8023  000AA4  002

$.TEST    000000  000000  0182F4  00D

Disk compacted 000 free sectors
```

This verified that the dummy file of 635 records had completely filled the space available on the disk.

Similarly, to find the size of the file we have just created we could have simply typed *INFO TEST, in which case the screen display would have been

```
*INFO TEST

$.TEST    000000  000000  0182F4  00D
```
                                    ↑
                                    File size in hexadecimal

The file size can be converted to decimal as discussed previously.

65536s	4096s	256s	16s	1s
1	8	2	F	4

Noting that F represents 15 in decimal we have

```
 1 × 65536 = 65536
 8 × 4096  = 32768
 2 × 256   =   512
15 × 16    =   240
 4 × 1     =     4
             _____
             99060 characters
```

The file therefore has a length of 99060 characters.

This could also be obtained, much more simply, by entering (in immediate mode)

`X = OPENUP "TEST": PRINT EXT#X`

and the extent of the file (99060 bytes) is displayed.

These calculations have shown that a file of 99060 characters has been created and this of course is identical to the number of records × record length i.e. 635 × 156.

Thus we can see that the user has complete control over the allocation of disk space to files, the ability to fully utilise the available space and to pinpoint the exact position of a single character.

Towards a Viable Data Base Program

Further it can be seen that we can handle a file of nearly 100K even though the available RAM (on the BBC Model B) is considerably less than its nominal 32K. On the Master 128 and 512, memory size is less critical, but the point is that files may be handled which greatly exceed the computer's memory. There is no need (in this case) for all of the records to reside in the memory simultaneously. Using 80 track disks of course, we can use files of twice the size—over 1200 records per file in this example. Winchester hard disks of 5–100 megabytes transform data handling into a different world with greater speed and capacity, but at a greater cost.

The complete program

Together with ideas covered earlier in this book, the features such as truncating, padding and dummy records are built into a complete program (Fig. 11.3). As this is rather a lengthy program I have resorted to the use of multi-statement lines, although only, I hope, for short statements which are easy to follow. After the complete program annotated listings of the various parts of the program are given.

```
100    ON ERROR CLOSE#0:GOTO 270
110  REM:THE RECORD FORMAT
120  REM:field$(N)=FIELD NAME
130  REM:length(N)=FIELD LENGTH
140  REM:record=RECORD LENGTH
150  REM:data$(N)=FIELD DATA
160  DIM field$(10),length(10),data$(10)
170  FOR N=0 TO 9
180     READ field$(N),length(N)
190     record=record+length(N)
200     NEXT:record=record+20
210  DATA NAME,30,ADDRESS,28,D. OF B.,8
220  DATA DESCRIPTION,10,QUALIFICATIONS,9
230  DATA NAT.INS.NO,9,DATE JOINED,8
240  DATA SALARY,6,PREVIOUS EMPLOY,20
250  DATA DATE LEFT,8
260
270  REPEAT:PROCmenu
280     IF option=1 THEN PROCcreate
290     IF option=2 THEN PROCscan
300     IF option=3 THEN PROCnumber_search
310     IF option=4 THEN PROCname_search
320     IF option=5 THEN PROCappend
330     UNTIL option=6:END
340
350  DEF PROCmenu:CLS
360  PRINT TAB(4,6);"1:Create a New File"
370  PRINT TAB(4,8);"2:Scan an Entire File"
380  PRINT TAB(4,11);"Read/Modify a Single Record"
390  PRINT TAB(4,12);STRING$(27,"-")
400  PRINT TAB(4,13);"3:Search on Record No."
410  PRINT TAB(4,15);"4:Search using Name"
420  PRINT TAB(4,18);"5:Append a Record"
430  PRINT TAB(4,20);"6:End this Run"
440  PRINT'"Please  Enter the Option Number"
450  PRINT"(In the Range 1_6 inclusive)"
```

Fig. 11.3 A program to create and maintain data files using fixed length fields and random access

The complete program 111

```
460 option=GET-48:ENDPROC
470
480 DEF PROCcreate:CLS
490 INPUT'"GIVE THE FILE A NAME "file$
500 X=OPENOUT file$
510 REPEAT:PROCenter
520    UNTIL string$="***"
530 REM WRITING 20 DUMMIES
540 FOR T=1 TO 20:FOR N=0 TO 9
550      PRINT#X,STRING$(length(N),"*")
560      NEXT N:NEXT T
570 CLOSE#X:ENDPROC
580
590 DEF PROCenter:CLS:PRINT'''
600 FOR N=0 TO 9:PROCinput
610    IF string$="***" THEN N=9
620    NEXT N
630 IF string$="***" THEN ENDPROC
640 PROCcheck:PROCwrite:ENDPROC
650
660 DEF PROCinput
670 PRINT field$(N);:INPUT string$
680 IF string$="***"THEN ENDPROC
690 string$=LEFT$(string$,length(N))
700 pad=length(N)-LEN(string$)
710    data$(N)=string$+STRING$(pad,CHR$32)
720 ENDPROC
730
740 DEF PROCcheck
750 REPEAT:PROCprint
760    PRINT'"IS RECORD OKAY-Y OR N ?"
770    G$=GET$
780    IF G$="N" OR G$="n"THEN PROCmodify
790    UNTIL G$="Y" OR G$="y":ENDPROC
800
810 DEF PROCprint:CLS:PRINT''
820 FOR N=0 TO 9
830    PRINT STR$(N);".";field$(N);":";
840    PRINTdata$(N):NEXT:ENDPROC
850
860 DEF PROCwrite:FOR N=0 TO 9
870    PRINT#X,data$(N)
880    NEXT:ENDPROC
890
900 DEF PROCread
910 FOR N=0 TO 9
920    INPUT#X,data$(N)
930    NEXT:ENDPROC
940
950 DEF PROCmodify
960 PRINT'"FIELD NO. TO BE MODIFIED ?"
970 REPEAT:N=GET-48:UNTIL N>=0 AND N<=9
980 PROCinput:ENDPROC
990
1000 DEF PROCscan:CLS
1010 INPUT'"ENTER THE FILE NAME "file$
```

Fig. 11.3 (continued)

```
1020 X=OPENIN file$:count=0
1030 REPEAT:count=count+1:PROCread
1040   IF data$(0)=STRING$(length(0),"*")THEN 1090
1050   PROCprint
1060   PRINTTAB(1,1);"RECORD NO :"count
1070   PRINT TAB(8,20)"PRESS SPACE TO CONTINUE"
1080   REPEAT UNTIL GET=32
1090   UNTIL data$(0)=STRING$(length(0),"*")
1100 CLOSE#X:ENDPROC
1110
1120 DEF PROCappend:CLS
1130 INPUT'''"ENTER THE FILE NAME "file$
1140 X=OPENUP file$
1150 REPEAT
1160   pointer=PTR#X:PROCread
1170   UNTIL data$(0)=STRING$(length(0),"*")
1180 PTR#X=pointer:PROCenter
1190 CLOSE#X:ENDPROC
1200
1210 DEF PROCnumber_search:CLS
1220 INPUT'''"ENTER FILENAME "file$
1230 X=OPENUP file$
1240 INPUT'''"ENTER RECORD NO. "number
1250 PTR#X=(number-1)*record
1260 pointer=PTR#X:PROCread:PROCcheck
1270 PTR#X=pointer:PROCwrite
1280 CLOSE#X:ENDPROC
1290
1300 DEF PROCname_search:CLS
1310 INPUT'''"ENTER FILENAME "file$
1320 X=OPENUP file$
1330 INPUT''"ENTER SEARCH NAME "search$
1340 REPEAT:pointer=PTR#X:PROCread
1350   IF LEFT$(data$(0),LEN(search$))<>search$ THEN 1370
1360   PROCcheck:PTR#X=pointer:PROCwrite
1370   UNTIL data$(0)=STRING$(length(0),"*")
1380 CLOSE#X:ENDPROC
1390
```

Fig. 11.3 (continued)

The program in detail

The complete program is shown in Fig. 11.3. No new ideas are incorporated—it is mainly an assembly of procedures described earlier in this book. The statement ON ERROR CLOSE#0:GOTO 270 closes the files and returns the user to the menu in the event of a genuine mistake or the ESCAPE key being pressed. It is advisable not to enter this line until the program has been tested, since it has the effect of suppressing any error messages.

1 Specifying the fields

Lines 160–250 are the lines which allow the program to be modified to suit any applica-

The program in detail 113

tion. For any file containing 10 fields per record, only lines 210–250 need to be altered to re-specify the field names and field lengths.

```
160 DIM field$(10),length(10),data$(10)
170 FOR N=0 TO 9
180   READ field$(N),length(N)
190   record=record+length(N)
200   NEXT:record=record+20
210 DATA NAME,30,ADDRESS,28,D. OF B.,8
220 DATA DESCRIPTION,10,QUALIFICATIONS,9
230 DATA NAT.INS.NO,9,DATE JOINED,8
240 DATA SALARY,6,PREVIOUS EMPLOY,20
250 DATA DATE LEFT,8
```

Fig. 11.4 The field specification for the personnel file

2 Changing the application

For a program not requiring 10 fields per record, the statements FOR N = 0 TO 9 would need to be altered throughout the program. While it would be more user friendly to specify the field names and lengths through a separate data file, DATA statements are used here for simplicity. For example, to change the application to suit the operating theatre equipment list mentioned previously, it would only be necessary to alter lines 210–250 and resave the program. A sample record for a typical operation was as follows:

```
0.OPERATION:LAPAROTOMY
1.TRAY:LARGE BASIC
2.EX.TRAY:GASTRO INT
3.EXTRAS:BALFOUR SR
4.BLADES:10X2
5.SUTURES:441
6.TIES:0 LINEN
7.POSITION:SUPINE
8.DRAINS:STERIVAC
9.POST OP:N.B.M 02
```

Fig. 11.5 A sample record for the operating theatre

Analysis of a number of records showed that the following field names and field lengths would be adequate.

Table 11.3

FIELD NO.	FIELD NAME	FIELD LENGTH
0	OPERATION	30
1	TRAY	28
2	EX.TRAY	20
3	EXTRAS	35
4	BLADES	6
5	SUTURES	15
6	TIES	10
7	POSITION	15
8	DRAINS	10
9	POST OP	15

Adapting the program for this application rather than the personnel file previously given

114 Towards a Viable Data Base Program

requires only the modification of the data statements 210–250 as follows:

```
210 DATA OPERATION,30,TRAY,28,EX.TRAY,20
220 DATA EXTRAS,35,BLADES,6
230 DATA SUTURES,15,TIES,10
240 DATA POSITION,15,DRAINS,10
250 DATA POST OP,15
```
Fig. 11.6

Note that the field number is supplied throughout the program in statements of the type FOR N = 0 to 9.

3 Record length

The total record length is calculated as the field lengths are read into the array *length(N)* by the statement:

```
record = record + length(N)
```

To allow for the fact that each of the 10 fields is extended by two bytes when written to disk, a further 20 bytes must be added to each record by the statement (Fig. 11.3).

```
record = record + 20
```

The variable *record* plays a crucial role in the remainder of the program, since it is used for calculation of pointer position in the random access options of the program e.g.

```
1250 PTR#X = (number-1)*record
```

4 The Menu

Accessing the various procedures via the menu is the same as discussed in previous programs, the options being as follows:

```
1:Create a New File
2:Scan an Entire File
Read/Modify a Single Record
------------------------------
3:Search on Record No.
4:Search using Name
5:Append a Record
6:End this Run


Please  Enter the Option Number
(In the Range 1_6 inclusive)
```
Fig. 11.7 The Menu

The only new feature about option 1 to Create a New File is the writing of 20 dummy records as shown in Fig. 11.8.

```
530 REM WRITING 20 DUMMIES
540 FOR T=1 TO 20:FOR N=0 TO 9
550     PRINT#X,STRING$(length(N),"*")
560     NEXT N:NEXT T
```
Fig. 11.8 Writing dummy records to the end of a new file

The program in detail 115

Obviously the user may wish to alter the number of dummy records to suit the particular application. Alternatively this could be programmed to be INPUT by the user. Note that each dummy record consists of ten fields (0–9), of *length(N)* as defined by the record specification given in lines 210–250.

Since the first dummy field at the end of the genuine data will consist of a set of asterisks corresponding to STRING$(length(0),"*"), this can be used as an end of (genuine) data marker. This is done during PROCscan, which works through the whole file, terminating with

```
1090 UNTIL data$(0) = STRING$(length(0),"*")
```

5 Entering the data

A new file is created during PROCenter. Entry of records is terminated when the user types "***" as field 0. Single records are entered during PROCinput which truncates and pads the fields as discussed previously using LEFT$ and STRING$. Note that option 1 can only be used once with a given file name, since OPENOUT will destroy any previous file with the same name.

A new feature included in this program is PROCcheck, which displays a newly entered record for inspection and correction before being written to disk.

```
740 DEF PROCcheck
750 REPEAT:PROCprint
760    PRINT'"IS RECORD OKAY-Y OR N ?"
770    G$=GET$
780    IF G$="N" OR G$="n"THEN PROCmodify
790    UNTIL G$="Y" OR G$="y":ENDPROC
```

Fig. 11.9 Displaying a record on the screen after entering at the keyboard, but before writing to disk

The record is displayed by PROCprint. If the user is satisfied, Y or y is entered and the record is written to disk.

```
0.OPERATION:AORTIC ANEURYSM
1.TRAY:LARGE BASIC
2.EX.TRAY:ARTERIAL
3.EXTRAS:PLED.SLINGS.HEP
4.BLADES:10
5.SUTURES:6/OPRO
6.TIES:193 194
7.POSITION:TRENDELENBERG
8.DRAINS:STERIVAC
9.POST OP:PU FPUL

IS RECORD OKAY-Y OR N ?
```

Fig. 11.10 The record displayed for inspection/modification

The record may not be satisfactory for two reasons:

1 An error may have occurred in typing the data.
2 Truncation to the specified field length may result in an unsatisfactory abbreviation.

116   Towards a Viable Data Base Program

In this case, the typing of N or n will cause PROCmodify to be called:

```
950 DEF PROCmodify
960 PRINT'"FIELD NO. TO BE MODIFIED ?"
970 REPEAT:N=GET-48:UNTIL N>=0 AND N<=9
980 PROCinput:ENDPROC
```

Fig. 11.11   Modifying a single field

The user enters the number of the field to be modified (in the range 0–9). The correct field data is then entered in PROCinput and truncated and padded. The complete record is again displayed for correction if necessary. When all of the fields are correct the record is written to disk in PROCwrite.

PROCread, PROCwrite and PROCscan contain no new ideas, except the use of the FOR ... NEXT loop to hold the data for the 10 fields (0–9) in the array *data$(N)*.

6   Updating the file

The real value of using a computer system to maintain a file of records is the ability to

1   Find a record quickly
2   Alter just a single field.

7   Random access via the record number

This is achieved in the program (Fig. 11.12) by DEF PROC*number_search*. It is necessary to know the record number so that the pointer position can be calculated by the previously described formula.

```
PTR#X = (number-1)*record
```

The variable *number* is the record number, and it is suggested that when a new file is created, a complete scan is printed on paper. This includes the printing of record numbers and the printout could then be used for reference when modifying the file.

After finding the required record by random access, it is read and modified if necessary, by PROCread and PROCcheck. Note that a variable store called *pointer* is used to hold the value of PTR#X before the record is read. This can then be used to reset the pointer to the required position for overwriting the old record by the modified version.

```
1210 DEF PROCnumber_search:CLS
1220 INPUT'''"ENTER FILENAME "file$
1230 X=OPENUP file$
1240 INPUT'''"ENTER RECORD NO. "number
1250 PTR#X=(number-1)*record
1260 pointer=PTR#X:PROCread:PROCcheck
1270 PTR#X=pointer:PROCwrite
1280 CLOSE#X:ENDPROC
```

Fig. 11.12   Locating and modifying a record using random access via the record number

8   Searching using a name

If the record number is not known then the user must enter a name and the program will search through the file until the name is found. The method of searching is therefore *sequential* but, unlike a cassette-based file, it is still possible to modify a single record and an individual field within it. The search has been programmed using LEFT$ so there is a wildcard element to it. (Fig. 11.13). The search works only on field(0) but modification to search on more than one field is simply a case of extending line 1350 to include *data$(1), data$(2)* etc.

So if, for example, we cannot remember how to spell a name like tracheotomy, simply typing tra would find all operations beginning with these letters. The store *search$* would contain tra, LEN(search$) would be 3, so the file would be scanned for all records whose first field begins with these 3 letters.

The opportunity is then given to check and modify the record before it is written to the disk. Again *pointer* is used to hold and reset the value of the pointer PTR#X at the beginning of the record, prior to writing the modified record.

```
1300 DEF PROCname_search:CLS
1310 INPUT'''"ENTER FILENAME "file$
1320 X=OPENUP file$
1330 INPUT'''"ENTER SEARCH NAME "search$
1340 REPEAT:pointer=PTR#X:PROCread
1350   IF LEFT$(data$(0),LEN(search$))<>search$ THEN 1370
1360   PROCcheck:PTR#X=pointer:PROCwrite
1370   UNTIL data$(0)=STRING$(length(0),"*")
1380 CLOSE#X:ENDPROC
```

Fig. 11.13 Locating and modifying a record by searching for a name

Notice that the search will need to proceed through the entire file of genuine records. We therefore continue the search until the first dummy is encountered i.e.

```
1370 UNTIL data$(0) = STRING$(length(0),"*")
```

> N.B. Modifying a file using OPENUP can only be carried out on later machines, supplied with BASICII. This can be examined by typing REPORT.
> If "(c)1982 Acorn" appears then OPENUP will work on your machine. If 1981 appears then the command to use for modifying a file is OPENIN. In this case all programs containing OPENUP must be modified by replacing with OPENIN.

9 Appending a record

To add a record to the end of the file it is simply a case of reading to the first dummy record. This is then overwritten by the genuine record which is to be appended.

```
1120 DEF PROCappend:CLS
1130 INPUT'''"ENTER THE FILE NAME "file$
1140 X=OPENUP file$
1150 REPEAT
1160   pointer=PTR#X:PROCread
1170   UNTIL data$(0)=STRING$(length(0),"*")
1180 PTR#X=pointer:PROCenter
1190 CLOSE#X:ENDPROC
```

Fig. 11.14 Appending a record after searching for the dummy record

118 *Towards a Viable Data Base Program*

Suggestions for further work

Further improvements may be made to this program such as the addition of colour and more instructions for the user. If the search for a name is not successful it would be helpful to print a message such as "NAME NOT FOUND" before returning to the menu.

The reader should note that when a large number of records are involved, it is very much faster to search by record number than by searching for a name. During testing of a file containing 600 records I searched for record 500 by both methods, and the results are shown in Table 11.4.

Table 11.4. Comparisons of searching time for sequential and random methods of access

Method used	Time to find 500th record
Search using name	187 seconds
Search on record number	2 seconds

However, even if it is necessary to use the sequential search for a name, it is then a simple matter to modify the record. This is a far superior method to sequential filing where the entire file must be rewritten. It is also vastly superior to the manual method where sheets of paper would need to be completely retyped to provide up-to-date lists.

Another improvement to the program would be the creation of a small file to enable the user to enter the field names and field lengths, rather than use the DATA statements method described.

In addition, **validation** checks could be built into the program to ensure that the data entered was suitable and within reasonable limits. This, of course, would be specific to a particular application and so it is not relevant to the program given which is meant to have almost universal applications (except for the need to change DATA statements 210–250).

The user may enter and RUN this program with confidence—it has been tried and tested by many people on a variety of subjects. It is of course necessary to choose file names which do not exceed 7 letters—and obviously the shorter the better from the typing point of view.

Two final steps may be added to protect the program and make it easier to load. The first is to lock the program, preventing accidental deletion. My program, called "FIX" (since it created fixed length fields) is locked by the statement

*ACCESS FIX L

If it is later necessary to unlock the program to modify it then this can be achieved by

*ACCESS FIX

A further precaution, in addition to locking the program, would be to make a backup copy on another disk. It might also be write-protected by sticking one of the special tabs provided with a new disk, over the rectangular slot on the disk. Of course this would then require the actual data files to be recorded on a disk separate from the program disk.

To save typing CH."FIX" to load and run the program, it may be created as a "BOOT" file on the disk. It can then be chained by simply holding down SHIFT and briefly pressing

Suggestions for further work

BREAK. To achieve this type

```
*BUILD:0.$.!BOOT

1 CHAIN "FIX"

2         (PRESS ESCAPE)
```

and then enter

```
*OPT 4,3
```

Henceforth this particular disk will always load and run the program called "FIX" whenever it is 'booted' using SHIFT and BREAK.

APPENDIX 1

A GLOSSARY OF TERMS USED IN DATA HANDLING WITH BBC MICROCOMPUTERS

Algorithm This is the method or set of rules needed to perform a particular task. The algorithm is derived without reference to any programming language. For example, the basic method for the Shell sort is quite independent of any computer language — it could be applied to a set of cards to be sorted by hand.

Array A large number of different items of data falling within the same category may be stored in a set of stores with a single name. Individual members of the array are distinguished by subscripts appended to the variable name.

Variable Name	Sample Data
make$(1)	FORD
make$(2)	BMW
make$(3)	RENAULT
make$(4)	PORSCHE

The first 4 elements of the array *make$(N)*. All arrays must be DIMensioned once, and only once, at the beginning of the program. See also '**Subscripts**'.

ASCII Code The American Standard Code for Information Interchange. The digits 0–9, upper and lower case letters, symbols and punctuation marks are represented in most computers by the same set of codes; e.g. the letter A is 65 and the number 1 is 49. These codes may be examined using the GET function, GET taking the ASCII code of the key pressed.

```
e.g.   10 code=GET
       20 PRINT code
       30 GOTO 10
```

Backing Store The magnetic storage medium on which programs and data are permanently recorded. Floppy disks and Winchester hard disks are the most suitable for microcomputers, with cassettes being a cheap but greatly inferior alternative. Cassettes cannot be considered seriously for business use as they are very slow and lack the sophisticated file handling facilities offered by disks.

Appendix 1: A Glossary of Terms 121

BASIC	Beginners All-purpose Symbolic Instructional Code. The language most widely used in personal computers, it is particularly suitable for educational and small business use.
BOOT	A quick method of loading and running a program which has been designated as the BOOT file on a disk. Only SHIFT and BREAK need to be pressed to run the program.
Byte	A set of eight bits (binary digits 0's and 1's representing a character such as the letter P, the number 7 or a punctuation mark such as ;
Character	A number (0–9 inclusive), upper or lower case letter, symbol and also a space.
Constant	A number or a string of characters to be stored in a named memory location e.g.

```
LET score = 17        LET name$ = "SMITH"
```

The actual number 17 and the string "JONES" are constants—they never change. However, the contents of the stores named *score* and *name$* can be overwritten by fresh data, and the stores are therefore called variables.

Daisywheel	A type of printer used when high quality text is more important than speed (e.g. for business letters). The daisywheel consists of characters arranged on the ends of radial arms or 'petals'. For large quantities of program listings and printed output, the dot-matrix printer is more suitable.
Data	Facts, figures, words or characters, input in a 'raw' or unprocessed form, to be converted by the computer into meaningful information.
Data Base	A large collection of files. One program might gain access to several of the files in a data base using a hierarchy of menus and passwords for security. Many large commercial data bases residing in mainframe computers can now be accessed by BBC microcomputers, e.g. Prestel.
Documentation	A complete, written description of a program including the purpose, program listings, sample input, output and operating instructions. Documentation should be clear, non-technical and should enable personnel other than the originator to use the program and modify it if necessary.
Dot-matrix	A type of printer commonly used for general purpose computing work i.e. program listings and output where high quality is not of paramount importance. 'Near letter quality' dot-matrix printers are available. Each character is formed by the selection of a particular combination of ink dots arranged in a rectangular matrix on the moving print head.
Field	An individual piece of data within a record; e.g. a record consisting of the name and address of one person might have 5 separate fields of name, house, street, town, postcode.

122 *Appendix 1: A Glossary of Terms*

File A collection of records such as the customers of a small business—one record being the details of one particular customer.

Floppy disk Magnetic disk, commonly $5\frac{1}{4}''$ or $3\frac{1}{2}''$ diameter, on which data is stored on concentric tracks, permitting high speed recording and retrieval of data. Single-sided 40 track disks for the BBC machine can hold 100K of data while double-sided 80 track disks have a capacity of 400K per disk. Dual disk drives can therefore hold up to 800K with the advantage of very rapid copying of disks. Disk storage is much faster, but more expensive than cassette tape.

GIGO Garbage in, garbage out—a reminder that mistakes are invariably caused by inaccurate entering of programs and data, not by the computer itself.

Grandfather–father–son system When files are frequently updated with new records, etc. it is normal to keep, for security purposes, the last three in the line of development—the earliest version being the 'grandfather'—the latest the 'son'. When a new son is 'born' the previous grandfather can be erased.

With this system, should the current father or son be accidentally lost or destroyed they could be reconstructed, provided details of the modifications have been kept.

It is normal to make duplicate copies of important disks and store them in a different geographical location from the originals.

Files and programs may also be **locked** to prevent accidental deletion.

Hacker This is a recent phenomenon—sometimes called the 'electronic burglar'. The hacker is an enthusiast armed with a microcomputer and modem. A common offence is to attempt to gain unauthorised entry to mainframe computers. When discovered, the hacker frequently claims to be merely drawing attention to the weaknesses in the security of the system. However, it is claimed that hacking is attracting the attention of organised crime, realising the potential for computer fraud such as electronic fund transfer. Hacking appears to be an exclusively male pastime.

Hard copy This is the output from the computer, printed on paper rather than as a screen display. Program listings may be studied at leisure away from the computer, providing a more efficient method of program development and modification.

Continuous stationery employs a **tractor feed** mechanism in the printer, drawing the paper by means of small sprocket teeth which engage in holes at the edge of the paper. **Friction feed** printers accommodate single sheets gripped between rollers.

For large quantities of standardised output, pre-printed stationery may be used to allow variable output generated by the computer to appear in a standard format such as a wage slip or a bill.

Another type of stationery consists of address labels which are supplied on a backing of continuous tractor feed paper. A complete mailing list stored on file can easily be printed in one operation, representing a great saving in time over traditional methods.

Hard disk This is a single fixed disk capable of servicing the needs of an entire college, school or small/medium business. Winchester hard disk drives typically have capacities of 10, 20 or 30 megabytes. Sophisticated security systems require a system manager, passwords and user numbers with different levels of user status, and accounting systems for the allocation of disk space.

A typical system may allow approximately 255 users and a total storage capacity more than 40 times greater than the 800K floppy disk drive (1 megabyte ≈ 976K).

Hardware The metal, plastic, silicon components of the computer.

Information The final output from the computer after processing, which may have included sorting or calculating. Information implies facts which are meaningful to the reader.

INPUT	PROCESS	OUPUT
Raw Data		Meaningful Information

K (Kilobyte) The unit of memory capacity — 1k is 1024 (or 2^{10}) characters.

Listing A display on the VDU or printer of all of the lines of the program currently in the memory.

Loop A section of a program whose instructions are repeated until some condition is satisfied. Usually achieved by FOR ... NEXT and on BBC machines also by REPEAT ... UNTIL.

Machine Code The internal language of the computer, consisting of combinations of 0s and 1s, enabling instructions, calculations, sorting and storing of data to be performed, e.g. the letter C is often 1000011, the figure 7 is 0110111.

Megabyte A million bytes—nearly 1000K. Hard disk systems may have a capacity of 10, 20 or 30 etc. megabytes (mb).

Menu A list of options displayed on the screen, from which the user may choose to run any one of several independent procedures. The user is then returned to the menu to make a further choice. If the menu started at line 1000, say, then the statement

```
ON ERROR GOTO 1000
```

would return the user to the menu rather than break out of the program with an error message.

Modem A device which connects a microcomputer to a telephone line enabling data, text and programs to be transmitted and received nationally or internationally. See also **Network**.

Network A network may exist, in its most localised form, as a group of BBC microcomputers linked together in one room to give shared access to a disk drive (800K or Winchester hard disk) and printers. A larger system may extend to work stations scattered around a college or company premises.

124 *Appendix 1: A Glossary of Terms*

Communication, nationally or internationally, is obtained by connecting the micro to the telephone lines via a modem. The network is created by the formation of a closed user group—fee paying subscribers to the system. All communication between users is via the host company's mainframe computer. Each user is allocated an identity number and mailbox (in the mainframe) and electronic mail may be 'deposited' provided the recipients identity number is known. However, to read the mail it is also necessary to know the password of the mailbox—which is 'user-defined' and may be changed at any time by the owner of the box. Such a network may be used to 'upload' (send) or 'download' (receive) not only text, but programs, files and information from a commercial data base such as Prestel.

At the time of writing, the protection of mailboxes by a user identity number and a password is not preventing hackers from gaining unauthorised access.

Peripherals	External devices, connected to the computer, e.g. printer, disk drive, modem, second processor.
PROCEDURE	A small, independent 'module' or block of a program, which is defined once, but may be called up and used frequently. Modular programs consist of a set of procedures accessed by a menu. Procedures are faster and more meaningful than their predecessor, the subroutine.
QWERTY	The standard layout of the letters on the keyboard of many computers (and typewriters).
RAM	Random Access Memory. That part of the computer's memory which is available to the user to 'write' to and 'read' from. **Shadow RAM** on the B+ and Master Series is an additional section of memory (20K) dedicated to the storage of the screen and its graphics, so releasing an equivalent amount for the user's programs. This additional RAM is situated adjacent to the main memory and is said to be in its 'shadow'.
Record	One set of data, within a file, such as the name and address of one person, or the recipe for one dish.
ROM	Read Only Memory. Part of the memory which contains *permanently* stored programs used in the operation of the machine—not available to the user for storing programs. Additional ROM chips may be fitted to an add-on ROM board to accommodate commercial software packages. These might include a word processor or an accountancy program.

(**EPROM**—erasable, programmable read only memory—may be reprogrammed by the user with specialist knowledge and equipment.)

The many ROM chips available for the BBC range of computers are all loaded into one section of main computer memory (but not all at the same time). The system of invoking or calling up a particular ROM into this area of memory is known as **paging**.

The Master Series includes as standard the View word processor ROM and the Viewsheet package for manipulating tabulator data as in the accountacy spreadsheet.

Appendix 1: A Glossary of Terms

Searching Scanning the data to identify those items which fulfil particular requirements:

e.g. IF A$(I) = "PORSCHE" THEN ....

Random access is much faster than sequential searching.

Second Processor This is a peripheral unit which plugs into the Tube interface of the BBC microcomputer. The two most common second processors are the Z80 or a further 6502. The main advantages of the second processor are more memory and faster program execution. On the Master Series, modular design enables further 'co-processors' to be fitted to the machine for ease of expandability. These co-processors provide either 16-bit or 32-bit computing and result in greater speed and memory than the standard 8-bit processor.

Software Programs and files, usually stored on disk or tape or ROM. Commercial programs for a particular application are known as **software packages**.

Sorting Arranging data in a particular order, usually alphabetical or numerical. The Bubble and Shell sorts are often used with microcomputers.

String A group of characters e.g. "CECIL" or "ABC123".

Structured Programming An attempt to write programs which are easy to follow and modify. This may be necessary in two situations:

1 A student trying to learn from a sample program.
2 A programmer inheriting someone else's work for development/correction.

Some features of structured programming include:

1 Generous spacing to highlight important sections of the program, e.g. using LISTO 7 before LIST, and blank lines to separate PROCEDURES.
2 Meaningful variable names.
3 Avoidance of multiple statement lines (where practicable).
4 Division of the program into clearly defined modules, accessed as PROCEDURES via a MENU.
5 Avoidance of branching using GOTO wherever possible, and never out of FOR ... NEXT, REPEAT ... UNTIL loops or PROCEDURES.

Subroutine A small section of a program which is frequently executed. Usually accessed by GOSUB line number and left by RETURN. Subroutines are available in BBC BASIC but are inferior to the faster and more meaningful PROCEDURES.

Subscript A number appended in brackets to a variable so that one variable name may uniquely identify a large **array** of stores e.g.

name$(1), name$(2), name$(3) ... name$(299), name$(300)

The presence of an array must always be announced (at the beginning

126 *Appendix 1: A Glossary of Terms*

of a program) by a DIMension statement (which must not be repeated).

Data could be read into an array by the lines:

```
100 DIM name$(300)
110 FOR I=1 TO 300
120 READ name$(I)
130 NEXT I
```

etc.

Syntax

The rules for the programming language, including spelling and punctuation e.g. the mis-spelt command PLINT instead of PRINT would produce a SYNTAX error, reported on the screen by the message 'Mistake'.

Terminator

In a set of DATA statements a 'dummy' field is included to mark the end of the data. This is then tested for during the READ module. Obviously the choice of dummy field must be so bizarre that it could never occur naturally in the data—otherwise the read operation would end too soon.

Typical end of data terminators might be

***, ZZZ or −999

The dummy data is used as the terminating condition in a loop.

```
100 REPEAT
110 I=I+1
120 READ name$(I)
130 UNTIL name$(I)="***"
```

Similarly, the end of a data file (as opposed to a block of DATA statements) can be detected using EOF# ..., as shown in the following example:

```
100 Y=OPENIN "TEST"
110 REPEAT
120 INPUT#Y,name$
130 PRINTname$
140 UNTIL EOF#Y
```

Text File

It is possible to carry out a very simple form of word processing using the BBC micrcomputer and disk drive. After entering the command *BUILD with a suitable file name, such as LETTER, the user enters the text at the keyboard e.g.

```
*BUILD LETTER

1 Dear John,

2 Thankyou for your recent letter.......
```

On completion of the entry of the text, the user presses ESCAPE to close the text file.

To read the text file back from disk, enter *TYPE LETTER and press RETURN. The text will be displayed on the screen or printed on paper. Note that although line numbers appear automatically

Appendix 1: A Glossary of Terms

while creating the text file with *BUILD, they do not reappear on reading with *TYPE.

The use of MODE 0 for this work gives compatibility between the screen and an 80 column printer.

Variable

The label given to a memory store, whose contents can be changed or overwritten and therefore *vary*. BBC BASIC allows meaningful variable names of unlimited length such as *cost, name$* etc. The omission of the $ sign means that only numeric data may be held in the store. The presence of the $ allows the handling of alphabetic and 'alphanumeric' data—a mixture of both letters and numbers. The data held in such stores is known as string data. While a number such as 19 might be held in an alphanumeric string store like *name$*, no mathematical work can be performed on it. The number will be stored only as a string of characters, 1 followed by 9, not as the mathematical number 19 between 18 and 20. To convert the string 'number' to the mathematical number, it must be preceded by VAL,

i.e. `VAL(name$)`

A string can be up to 255 characters long (1024 characters on the Master)

VDU

Visual Display Unit—the television or monitor screen on which programs and output are displayed. For business use, such as data and word processing, a monochrome screen may suffice, although graphical work may require a colour monitor.

Word processing

Sophisticated typewriting using a microcomputer. Text may be checked and corrected on the screen before committing to paper. Powerful editing facilities allow deletion and insertion of characters, lines, paragraphs or pages and the replacement of a word by another throughout the entire text.

Standard letters and files may be permanently stored on diskette for subsequent recall, **infilling** from a file of names and addresses to produce 'personalised letters' i.e. with no distinction in type quality between the infilled name and the rest of the letter. Multiple copies may be specified.

Aesthetic features include 'right justification'—all lines of text ending in a neat vertical column—and 'proportional spacing' e.g. letter 'i' not occupying as much space as the letter 'w'.

A word processing system consists of a standard BBC microcomputer, monitor, disk drive and printer. The word processor is itself a program usually stored on a ROM chip installed permanently inside the computer. Two well established programs for the BBC micro are View and Wordwise.

Serious word processing requires a disk drive, although cassette versions are available for the beginner. For general use a dot-matrix printer may be adequate but high quality business letters call for a 'daisywheel'.

Appendix 1: A Glossary of Terms

```
This piece of text was produced with Wordwise Plus
and a normal Epson RX80F/T Printer. You can see why
it is called Dot Matrix!
```

```
This paragraph was produced using the same printer
after invoking the Watford NLQ ROM installed in the
BBC Micro. The inevitable price for this higher
quality is a reduction in printing speed.
```

APPENDIX 2

Graphical Presentation of Data

This topic has been included as an appendix because it is of a more specialised and complex nature than the previous work. From experience I know that the mathematics involved will be an anathema to many people who may prefer to ignore the topic altogether. Alternatively, it is hoped that the short routines given may be useful as the basis of procedures which the reader may incorporate into much larger programs.

Visual presentation of statistics in the form of line graphs, bar charts and pie charts is a time-consuming task when performed manually and is an ideal application for a computing solution. The BBC DRAW, PLOT and colour facilities enable attractive presentations to be made; with suitable programming the relatively complex mathematical task of producing a pie chart may be reduced to an unskilled typing operation. The following programs show how it is feasible to enter raw, uncorrected figures at the keyboard and process them automatically to produce meaningful graphs. Such raw data might consist of a set of sales figures and the corresponding months in which they occur, or rainfall/temperature readings measured on a daily basis.

In this way the computer may be used 'on-line' to give visual presentations direct to one or more monitors; alternatively 'hard copy' graphical output on paper may be obtained with a printer and a suitable 'screen-dump'.

The algebra and trigonometry involved in the following work may be of little interest to the non-mathematical reader. In this case it is suggested that the reader skips such explanations and merely uses the sample programs as procedures to be copied and 'plugged' into other programs whenever necessary.

There are a few golden rules in presenting data for display in this way, to improve readability and avoid the accusation of 'lies, damned lies and statistics'.

- Start each scale from a true origin.
- Use as much of the screen as possible.
- Include a title and label the axes.

1 The line graph

Table A.1 shows the monthly sales for a fictitious small business. In the remainder of this chapter these sales will be referred to as RAW DATA.

130 Appendix 2: Graphical Presentation of Data

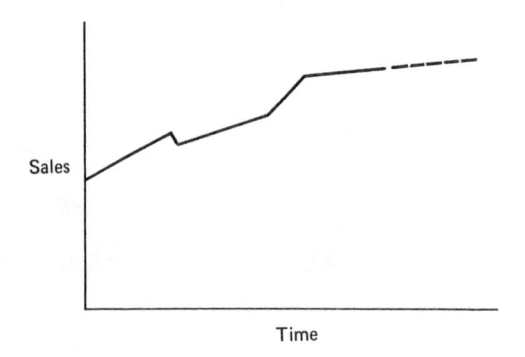

Fig. A.1 The line graph is commonly used to present data which varies with time, allowing predictions of future trends to be made

Table A.1

Month	JAN	FEB	MAR	APR	MAY	JUN	JUL	AUG	SEP	OCT	NOV	DEC
Sales	5437	3254	4168	2253	1367	828	437	1569	2396	4894	6396	8921

In all of the graphics modes, the layout of the BBC screen resembles a piece of graph paper with the origin in the bottom left-hand corner. There are 1280 addressable positions in the horizontal direction (0–1279 inclusive) and 1024 in the vertical direction (0–1023).

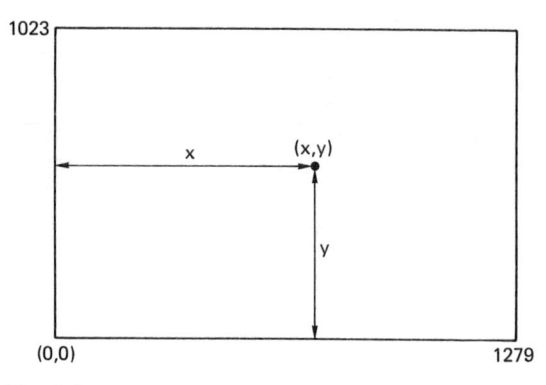

Fig. A.2 DRAW x,y draws a line absolutely (i.e. referred to screen position (0,0)

Redefining the origin

VDU 29 enables the origin to be positioned away from the default position at the bottom left-hand corner of the screen. To allow room for the axes to be drawn and labelled we will set the origin (0,0) at the position which was originally (100,100). This is achieved by the statement

```
VDU29,100;100;
```

Drawing the axes can then be accomplished by

```
MOVE 1100,0:DRAW 0,0:DRAW 0,800
```

1 The line graph

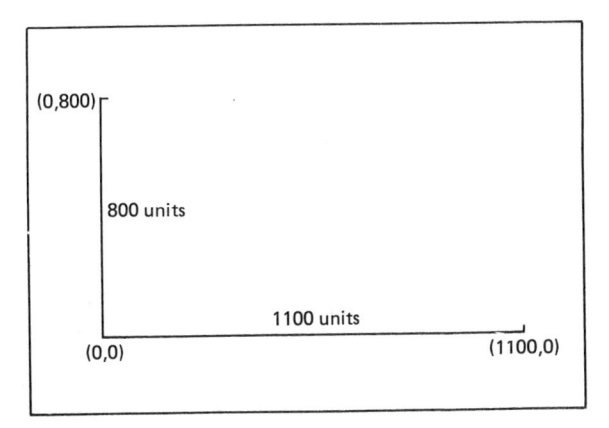

Fig. A.3 The positions of the axes referred to the new origin, after redefining using VDU 29

These new axes may be used for plotting any sort of numerical data; we simply scale the raw data to suit the available units on the screen. (The values of 800 and 1100 units were arrived at after allowing space for a title and labelling the scales.) Since we want the graph to occupy the whole of the axes, the 800 units on the vertical scale must cover the whole of the range of data to be plotted. In our sales example the range is £9000.

A suitable formula to obtain the y co-ordinate (vertical distance) of an individual point is as follows:

$$y = \frac{\text{raw data}}{\text{range}} \times 800$$

So sales of £4500 would give a y co-ordinate of

$$y = \frac{4500 \times 800}{9000} = 400 \text{ units}$$

The same method may be used to calculate the x co-ordinates, except that we have to scale a horizontal distance of 1100 units.

However, in many cases, such as the sales example shown, the horizontal scale will consist of a number of equal **intervals**, such as months or years. Successive x co-ordinates

$$\text{Interval} = \frac{1100}{(readings - 1)}$$

where *readings* is the number of readings to be plotted.

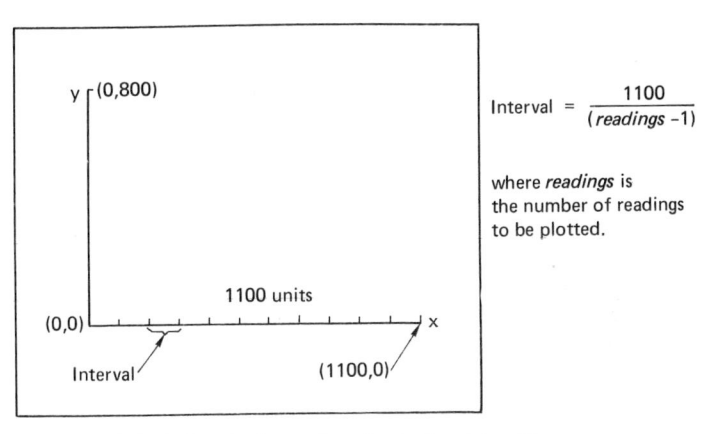

Fig. A.4 Calculating the interval on the horizontal scale

Appendix 2: Graphical Presentation of Data

can thus be obtained by incrementing the x co-ordinates by a statement such as

`x = x + interval`

With our monthly sales example, there are 12 'readings'. The results are to be plotted at 12 positions i.e. with 11 equal intervals.

Plotting the points

The points must be calculated in the program from the actual raw data (entered via INPUT) using the previously derived formulae. After drawing the y axis, we DRAW to the first point which will be at (0,y) and y will have been calculated. x is then incremented by the interval, the new y co-ordinate is calculated and we draw a line to it using DRAW(x,y). We continue entering raw data using a counter in the program to register the number of readings which have been entered by the user. The program ends when the value of the counter is the same as the total number of readings.

The following variable names have been used in the program (Fig, A.5):

- *vmax:* The maximum value on the vertical scale (£9000 in the current example).
- *readings:* The total number of readings to be plotted (12 in the current example).
- *interval:* The distance between successive readings on the horizontal scale (1100/11 = 100 in this example).
- *count:* The counter used to hold the number of readings which have been entered by the user at any time during the running of the program.

```
 20 REM INITIALISATION
 30 MODE 0
 40 VDU19,0,4,0,0,0
 50 PRINT TAB(5,1);"How many Readings"
 60 INPUT TAB(23,1);readings:CLS
 70 interval=1100/(readings-1)
 80 PRINTTAB(5,1);"Enter Max. Reading"
 90 PRINTTAB(5,2);"on the Vertical Scale"
100 INPUT TAB(26,2);vmax:CLS
110
120 REM Changing the Graphics Origin
130 VDU 29,100;100;
140
150 REM Drawing the Axes
160 MOVE 1100,0:DRAW 0,0:DRAW 0,800
170  FOR y=800 TO 200 STEP -200
180    MOVE 0,y:DRAW 20,y:NEXT y
190 MOVE0,0
200 FOR x=0 TO 1100 STEP interval
210    MOVE x,0:DRAW x,20:NEXT x
220
230 REM LABELLING THE SCALES
240 VDU5:MOVE -80,800:PRINT STR$(vmax)
250 MOVE -80,600:PRINT STR$(vmax*3/4)
260 MOVE -80,400:PRINT STR$(vmax/2)
270 MOVE -80,200:PRINT STR$(vmax/4)
280 MOVE -90,520:PRINT"SALES"
290 MOVE -60,470:PRINT"£"
```

Fig. A.5 A program to draw a line graph of monthly sales figures

```
300 FORx=-10 TO 1090 STEP interval
310    READ A$
320    MOVE x,-20:PRINT A$:NEXT x
330 DATA J,F,M,A,M,J,J,A,S,O,N,D
340
350 REM ENTERING AND PLOTTING THE DATA
360 MOVE 0,0:x=0:y=0 :VDU4
370 REPEAT
380    count=count+1
390    PROCinput
400    y=(data/vmax)*800
410    PROCdraw(x,y)
420    x=x+interval
430    UNTIL count=readings
440
450 PRINTTAB(20,1);"MONTHLY SALES FOR 1985"
460 PRINTTAB(20,2);"_____"
470 END
480
490 DEF PROCinput
500 INPUT TAB(5,1);"Enter a Reading "data
510 PRINT TAB(5,1);STRING$(25,CHR$(32))
520 ENDPROC
530
540 DEF PROCdraw(x,y)
550 DRAW x,y
560 ENDPROC
```

The program in detail

Initialisation

The complete program is shown in Fig. A.5. The first block (lines 10–100) is the initialisation stage, setting the various colours and variables. I have used Mode 0 for its high resolution and neat lettering. Although this is normally only a black and white mode, the colours can be changed by the VDU 19 statement.

The background is changed to blue by the statement

```
VDU 19,0,4,0,0,0
```

This statement means: change colour 0 (black) to colour 4 (blue). The display will now consist of white graphics on a blue background. Lines 50 and 60 enable the user to enter the total number of readings. In the monthly sales example, this is 12. The interval between plotted points is calculated at line 70. When the user is asked to "Enter Max. Reading ..." (lines 80–100), a rounded-up figure should be entered, say 9000 in our sales figures (Table A.1).

Drawing the axes

After changing the graphics origin at line 130, the axes are drawn as previously described. The FOR ... NEXT loops (lines 170–180) and (lines 200–210) produce graduation marks on the scales by drawing a series of short lines 20 units long.

Labelling the scales—using PRINT at the graphics cursor

To mark the vertical scale with maximum and quartile values, a greater degree of accuracy is needed than is possible using TAB(x,y). Instead, VDU 5 is used to enable accurate PRINTing at the graphics cursor on the 1280 × 1024 grid.

Line 240 accomplishes this precise printing. After the VDU 5 statement we move to position (−80,800). This is 80 units to the left of the vertical axis and level with the top. At this position we need to print the maximum reading on the vertical scale (*vmax*). In the current example this is 9000. However, if we PRINT *vmax*, since *vmax* is a number, it is printed at the right-hand side of a block of 10 characters—not at the precise position (−80,800). Fortunately, *strings* are printed on the left-hand side of a block of 10 characters so the problem is overcome by converting the number *vmax* to a string using STR$(vmax).

Intermediate values are placed on the vertical scale using *vmax* × 3/4, *vmax*/2, *vmax*/4, each time moving the cursor 200 units down the scale (since the entire vertical scale covers 800 units).

The previous statements may be used for line graphs on any subject. Lines 280 and 330 apply only to our monthly sales example and would need to be modified for other types of data. The word SALES and the £ sign are printed at suitable positions following the appropriate MOVE statements. The initials of the months of the year are supplied via READ and DATA and printed at the graphics cursor (lines 300–330).

Entering and plotting the DATA

Having drawn and labelled the axes we return to the origin (MOVE 0,0) at line 360. Printing using TAB(x,y) is restored by VDU 4.

PROCinput requests the user to "Enter a Reading" at which point individual readings from the table of sales figures are entered (enter one month's sales then press RETURN). The purpose of the mysterious line 510 is to wipe out previously entered numbers by printing 25 lots of character string 32 (spaces). After a reading has been entered into store *data* during PROCinput, it is scaled (line 400) to give the y value to be plotted:

```
y = (data/vmax)*800
```

The rather short PROCdraw draws a line to the required point. (PROCdraw is extended later in this chapter in the section on bar charts.)

Having drawn to the first point, x is incremented (line 420) by

```
x = x + interval
```

prior to the next month's sales figures being entered and plotted.

Note that when the program is RUN, nothing appears to happen after the first month's sales are entered and RETURN has been depressed. The program DRAWs to the required position, but since this is embedded in the y axis, no change appears on the screen. Entry of the second reading will however produce a line to the second point.

Entry and plotting of the data continues, the variable *count* holding the number of readings entered. When this value reaches the total number of readings in the data, the REPEAT ... UNTIL loop (line 430) is satisfied and DATA entry is terminated. Finally, the title of the graph is printed and underlined at lines 450 and 460.

The End statement at line 470 is necessary to prevent the procedures which follow from being entered erroneously i.e. without being called by a PROC statement.

When the program is entered and RUN using the data from Table A.1 the output is as shown in Fig. A.6.

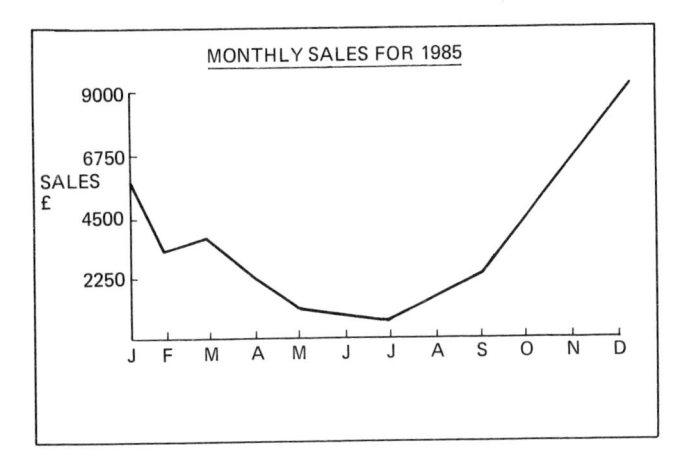

Fig. A.6 The screen output when the program (Fig. A.5) is run

Summary

The program demonstrated will allow any data to be plotted on horizontal and vertical axes, the axes being fixed by the program. The y co-ordinates are obtained by scaling, using the formula:

$$y = \frac{\text{actual data}}{\text{range}} \times 800$$

Although the horizontal scale was programmed to increment by a fixed interval of time in this case, values of x which do not increase by a fixed increment could easily be calculated from raw data by the formula:

$$x = \frac{\text{actual data}}{\text{range}} \times 1100$$

In the above formulae the true graphical origin (0,0) is at screen position (100,100). 800 and 1100 are the usable screen locations on the vertical and horizontal axes respectively.

While this example used white lines on a blue background in MODE 0 the reader may wish to experiment by altering the MODE and the appropriate colour statements as described in the User Guide.

Without further modification (except for the addition of suitable annotation such as titles), the previous program might be used for:

- Plotting of sales/profits/costs against time to predict future trends.
- Monitoring of variables such as rainfall, temperature, heartbeat, pollution levels (perhaps including horizontal tolerance lines to represent levels of acceptability/ rejection).
- Producing a graph of weight against time to compare the success or otherwise of dieting, also including a line to represent the target weight loss.

2 The bar chart

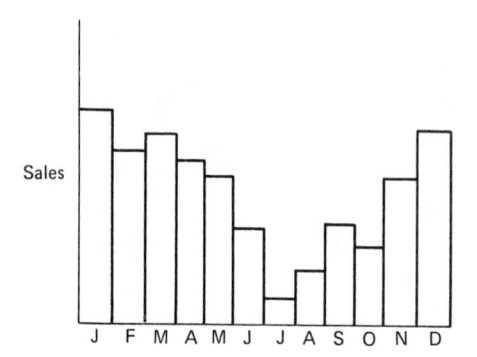

Fig. A.7 The bar chart is particularly useful for comparing the differences between readings

The previous data for monthly sales could also be drawn as a bar chart in addition to the line graph previously described. For the bar chart it is simply a case of drawing rectangular columns of height y and width equal to the interval. We will also fill in the column, using PLOT 85,x,y. (Users of the Master Series computers and also those fitted with the Acornsoft Graphics Extension ROM automatically have a 'flood-filling' facility for shading.)

When PLOT 85,x,y is used to plot to the point whose co-ordinates are (x.y), a triangle is shaded in the current foreground colour. The triangle is that formed by the point (x,y) and the last two points visited in previous DRAW or MOVE statements. Using PLOT 85, a variety of shapes may be infilled by 'tessellation' from a series of triangles.

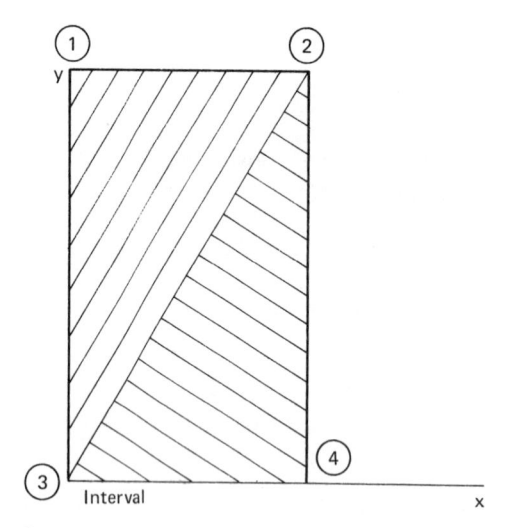

Fig. A.8

2 The bar chart

Modifying the program

The previous program (Fig. A.5) can easily be modified to present the monthly sales figures as a bar chart. Since we now require 2 separate columns along our horizontal scale of 1100 units, the interval calculation becomes:

```
70 interval = 1100/readings
```

where *readings* is the number of columns.

We now use *readings* not (*readings* − 1) as for the line graph. (12 columns require 12 intervals, whereas the 12 points on the line graph had only 11 intervals). To position the initials of the months on the horizontal scale in the centre of the columns, we must alter line 300 as follows:

```
300 FOR x = interval/2 TO 1100 STEP interval
```

Now we need to modify PROCdraw to infill the triangles.

```
540 DEF PROCdraw(x,y)
550 DRAW x,y
560 DRAW x+interval,y
570 PLOT 85,x,0
580 PLOT 85,x+interval,0
590 GCOL0,0
600 DRAW x,0
610 DRAW x,y
620 DRAW x+interval,y
630 DRAW x+interval,0
640 GCOL0,1
650 ENDPROC
```

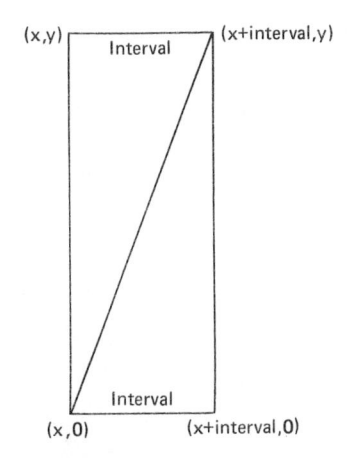

Fig. A.9 Shading the columns

Lines 550–570 DRAW and shade the upper triangle in the foreground colour (white). Line 580 shades the lower triangle, completing the rectangular column in white. In order to separate the individual columns they are outlined in the background colour (blue) in lines 590–630, in a series of DRAW statements. Line 590 sets the foreground colour to blue for this purpose, then it is restored to white by GCOL0,1 at line 640.

When the modified program is entered and RUN, the output is as shown in Fig. A.10.

138 *Appendix 2: Graphical Presentation of Data*

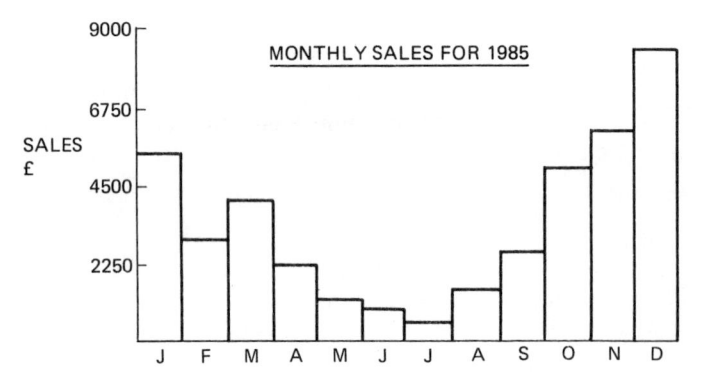

Fig. A.10 The screen output when the modified program is run

Summary

This program may be used for bar charts for any range of values on the vertical scale. Similarly, the program will cater for any number of columns along the horizontal scale, although new labels and titles will be needed for different subjects.

Suitable applications for this program might be:

- Sales/profits/losses on a monthly basis.
- Fuel consumption figures for different makes of car.
- Total scores of individual sportsmen over a season.

3 The pie chart

The pie chart is used when it is necessary to show how a fixed or finite total quantity is divided into its constituents. As an example let us consider the various species of fish in a pond at a given point in time. After netting the pond, the figures shown in Table A.2 might emerge.

Table A.2

Species	Number of Fish	Fraction of Total	Angle in Degrees
Roach	49	$\frac{49}{120}$	$\frac{49}{120} \times 360 = 147$
Perch	37	$\frac{37}{120}$	$\frac{37}{120} \times 360 = 111$
Bream	28	$\frac{28}{120}$	$\frac{28}{120} \times 360 = 84$
Pike	6	$\frac{6}{120}$	$\frac{6}{120} \times 360 = 18$
TOTAL	120	1	360

This data could be used to produce the pie chart of Fig. A.11.

3 The pie chart

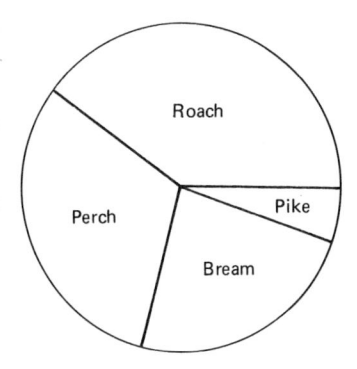

Fig. A.11 A pie chart to show the various proportions of the species of fish as a fraction of the total fish population of a pond

The example shown is a simple one, with only four 'slices' and carefully chosen numbers. With more complex data, the calculation is quite time-consuming and lends itself to a computing solution. The main problem is to draw the circle and this will require revision of some early trigonometry (Fig. A.12).

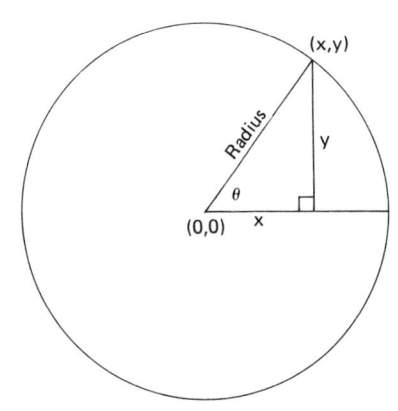

Assuming an origin of (0,0) anywhere on the screen, any point (x,y) on the circumference can be defined by:

y = radius * cos θ
y = radius * sin θ

Fig. A.12

Users of the Master series computers and also those fitted with the Acornsoft Graphic Extension ROM need only MOVE to the centre and PLOT to any point on the circumference.

Setting a new origin—VDU 29

To set the graphical origin (0,0) at the screen position 500,500, say, we will use
VDU 29,500;500;

Obtaining the angles

The computer uses radians rather than degrees for circular measure. The conversion is obtained from the fact that PI radians = 180° where PI = 3.14159265. Hence a complete

140   Appendix 2: Graphical Presentation of Data

circle covers approximately 6.283 or 2PI radians. A circle of any radius can therefore be drawn at position 500,500 by the following program:

```
 5   REM CIRCLE CENTRE (500,500)
10   MODE 2:VDU29,500;500;:GCOL0,1
20   INPUT"RADIUS"radius
30   FOR angle=0 TO 2*PI STEP 0.02
40      x=radius*COSangle:y=radius*SINangle
50      PLOT 69,x,y
60   NEXT angle
```

Fig. A.13 A program to draw a circle of any radius at position (500,500) on the screen

In the program, Fig. A.13, any radius may be INPUT, up to a maximum of 501 units, (since the centre is at (500,500)). Note that the STEP in line 30 may be altered to PLOT more or less points on the circumference.

Shading the slices

To distinguish between the 'slices' we will need to use different colours. We will increment the colour after each slice has been drawn. (Note the use of the lower case variable name *colour*.

e.g. `colour = colour + 1`

The next problem is to fill in the slices and for this we can laminate the slice from a series of radial spokes (Fig. A.14).

```
 5   REM DRAWING ONE SECTOR
10   MODE 2:VDU29,500;500;:GCOL0,1
20   INPUT"RADIUS"radius
30   INPUT"ANGLE"degrees
35   finish=degrees*PI/180
40   CLG:start=0
45   FOR angle=start TO finish STEP 0.01
50      x=radius*COSangle:y=radius*SINangle
60      MOVE 0,0:DRAW x,y
70   NEXT angle
```

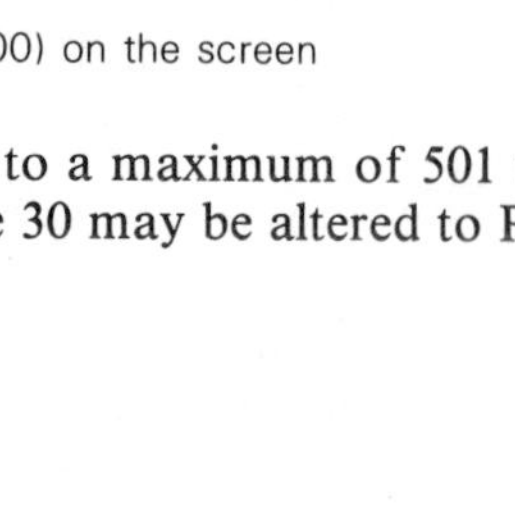

Each sector is laminated from a series of radial spokes

Fig. A.14 A program to DRAW one sector when the radius and angle are INPUT

This little routine may be extended to draw the complete pie chart by enclosing in a REPEAT ... UNTIL loop, to terminate when the final value of *finish* is 2PI. To obtain different colours we must insert *colour = colour* + 1. Note also that since each new slice must start where the previous one finished, we need to set *start* equal to *finish* after drawing each slice. The modified program is shown in Fig. A.15.

When the program (Fig. A.15) is RUN, the user must INPUT the radius (not greater than 400 units) and the angle in degrees. The program will truncate the final sector if it exceeds 2PI radians (360°).

So far we have developed a method of drawing the pie chart, given the sector angle as INPUT. To be really useful for practical applications, however, we need a program with

3 The pie chart   141

```
10    MODE2:VDU29,500;500;
20    INPUT "RADIUS"radius
30    CLG:start=0:colour=1
35
40    REPEAT
50       GCOL0,colour
55       PRINT TAB(10,2)"    "
60       INPUT TAB(5,2)"ANGLE"degrees
70       radians=degrees*PI/180
80       finish=radians+start
90       IF finish>2*PI THEN finish=2*PI
95
100      FOR angle=start TO finish STEP 0.01
110         x=radius*COSangle:y=radius*SINangle
120         MOVE 0,0:DRAWx,y
130      NEXT angle
135
140      start=finish:colour=colour+1
150   UNTIL finish=2*PI
```

Fig. A.15 A program to draw a PI chart in different colours for angles INPUT in degrees

the following specification:

- Allow raw data to be input.
- Permit any number of records to be input.
- Calculate the total and the sector angles.
- Draw pie chart in various colours.
- Present a key to relate the sectors to the data.

Referring to Table A.2 the data to be INPUT to produce our pie chart of fish stocks will be shown in Table A.3.

Table A.3

SPECIES	NUMBER
ROACH	49
PERCH	37
BREAM	28
PIKE	6

As this data needs to be retained in the memory, it will be stored in arrays *name$*(N) and *number*(N). After totalling the data, each number must be expressed as a fraction of the total fish stock. This fraction must be converted to an angle in radians by multiplying by 2π (or 2*PI in BBC BASIC). The pie chart is then drawn by the method used in the previous program (see Fig. A.16).

```
10    DIM name$(20),number(20)
20    MODE2:VDU 29,400;400;
30    COLOUR 3:COLOUR 132
40    N=0:total=0:count=0
50
60    REM ENTERING AND TOTALLING DATA
70    REPEAT
```

Fig. A.16 A program to draw pie charts from any number of records

142 Appendix 2: Graphical Presentation of Data

```
80     N=N+1:CLS
90     INPUT TAB(2,5)"ENTER NAME "name$(N)
100    IF name$(N)="***"THEN130
110    INPUT TAB(2,7)"ENTER NUMBER "number(N)
120    total=total+number(N):count=count+1
130    UNTIL name$(N)="***"
140
150    REM DRAWING THE SLICES
160    start=0:colour=0:GCOL0,128:CLG
170
180    FOR P=1 TO count
190       colour=colour+1:GCOL0,colour
200       radians=(number(P)/total)*2*PI
210       finish=radians+start
220
230       FOR angle=start TO finish STEP.01
240          x=300*COSangle:y=300*SINangle
250          MOVE 0,0:DRAW x,y
260       NEXTangle
270
280       start=finish
290
300    NEXTP
```

Fig A.16 (continued)

Raw data is entered, totalled and sector angles calculated before the pie chart is drawn. Data entry is terminated by typing "***" in response to "ENTER NAME".

The program in Fig. A.16 does not convey very much if there is no key to relate the sectors to the data. We will print the key at the graphics cursor, using VDU5. A suitable datum for the key is the point (800,950). Using DRAW and PLOT 85 statements a triangle is drawn from this position, and the name of the sector is printed in the appropriate colours. y is then decreased, the colour incremented and the second triangle and name are displayed in the appropriate colours e.g.

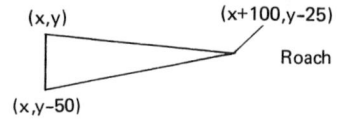

```
(x,y)            (x+100,y-25)
                          Roach
(x,y-50)
```

The additional lines of the program which accomplish this are shown in Fig. A.17.

```
320    REM RESET ORIGIN AT SCREEN (0,0)
330    VDU29,0;0;
340
350    REM TEXT AT GRAPHICS CURSOR
360    VDU5:x=800:y=950:colour=0
370
380    REM DRAWING THE KEY
390    FOR N=1 TO count
400       colour=colour+1:GCOL0,colour
410
420       REM DRAWING TRIANGLES
430       MOVE x,y:DRAW x+100,y-25
```

Fig. A.17 Drawing the triangles for the key, in the appropriate colour

```
440     PLOT85,x,y-50
450
460     REM KEY NAMES AT GRAPHICS CURSOR
470     MOVE x+130,y-10:PRINTname$(N)
480     y=y-150
490     NEXT N
500
510     REM SWITCH CURSOR OFF
520     VDU21
```

Fig. A.17 (continued)

The complete pie chart program is obtained by combining Figs. A.16 and A.17.

VDU29,0;0; in Fig. A.17 resets the graphics origin (0,0) to the bottom left-hand corner of the screen. VDU5 enables the text for the sector names to be written at the graphics cursor. *count* is the number of sectors in our data. *colour* is used to increment the graphical colour so that the triangle colours match those in the pie chart.

The triangles are actually drawn by the statements

```
430 MOVE x,y:DRAW x+100,y-25
```

```
440 PLOT 85,x,y-50
```

The triangles are printed down the screen, being moved by the statement $y = y - 150$.

Finally VDU21 prevents the cursor prompt from appearing on the screen.

If the complete program (Fig. A.16 + Fig. A.17) is entered and RUN, using the data from Table A.3, the pie chart and key will be displayed on the screen in various colours, as shown in Fig. A.18.

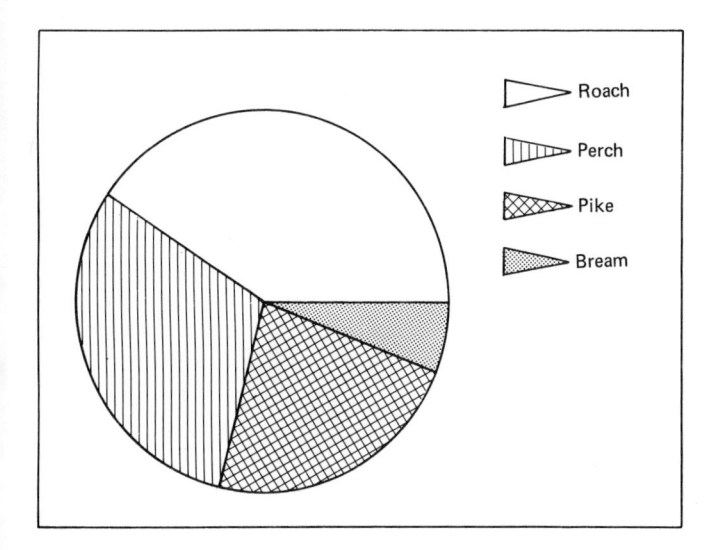

Fig. A.18 The screen display when the pie chart program is run using the data from Table A.3. The colours in MODE 2 will be red, green, yellow and blue

Summary

This program can be used to draw pie charts based on raw numbers on any topic, subject

144 Appendix 2: Graphical Presentation of Data

to the following limitations:

1 Any number of sectors may be used, but more than 7 will result in flashing colours for the eighth sector onwards.
2 The sector names e.g. roach, perch, etc. need to be restricted to about 6 characters maximum, with the existing screen layout.

Such a program will allow the user to produce pie charts on screen or paper, very much faster than by existing manual methods.

Suitable applications for this program might be:

- The contribution to group sales (or profits) made by the separate operating divisions within the group.
- The allocation of farmland to various activities such as beef, arable, dairying etc.
- The shares of the UK car market taken by various manufacturers.
- Any subject where there is a fixed total quantity and each constituent number can be expressed as a fraction of the whole.

Index

*Access, 78, 118
Acorn Master Series, 3
Advanced Disk Filing System (ADFS), 78
algorithm, 120
alphasort, 49
amending files, 67, 83
AND, 30
angles, 139
appending, 67, 83, 103, 117
arrays, 13, 120
ASCII code, 16, 27, 36, 96, 120
axes, 133

Backing store, 120
*BACKUP, 78, 88
bar chart, 136
BBC Micro, 3
BGET#, 96
BOOT file, 118, 121
bubble sort, 46
*BUILD, 119
byte, 77, 121

Calculation, 39
*CAT, 78
catalogue, 77, 92
character, 121
CHR$, 107
circle, 139
closing printer, 62
CLOSE#, 80, 98, 112
*COMPACT, 78, 108
constant, 121
*COPY, 78
counter, 12, 17, 59

Daisywheel, 121
data, 7, 72, 121
data base, 121
data files, 75

data handling, 3
DATA statement, 11, 12, 14, 33
decreasing loop, 53
delete, 67, 84, 103
*DELETE, 78, 88, 108
destination file, 88
dimension statement, 11
Disk Filing System (DFS), 77
DIV, 56
documentation, 121
double height letters, 62
DRAW (graphs), 133
dummy data, 12, 17, 33, 65, 71, 114

*ENABLE, 78, 88
*END statement, 21
end of data marker, 12, 23, 71
end of file (EOF#), 81, 88, 95
entering data, 11
EPROM, 121
EXT#, 95, 109
extending a program, 39

Field, 14, 66, 68, 82, 107, 112
file, 14, 75, 105, 108, 122
fixed length fields, 98, 107
floppy disk, 77, 122
formatting, 77
FOR...NEXT, 11, 12, 13, 44

GETS,GET$, 16, 19, 34
GIGO, 122
global variables, 41
grandfather – father – son, 122
greater than, 31

Hacker, 122
hard copy, 38, 62, 122
hard disk, 110, 123
hardware, 123

145

Index

hexadecimal, 108
hierarchical file structure, 79
holding store, 44, 63

IF...THEN..., 23, 30, 34, 66
immediate mode, 13, 42
*INFO, 109
information, 123
INKEY,INKEY$, 16
INPUT, 16, 23, 35, 81
INPUT#, 81, 83
insert, 67
integer variable, 12, 27, 51
interrogation, 22, 116

K(Kilobyte), 123
key field, 74

LEFT$, 27, 74
LEN, 28, 74, 107, 117
length of file (EXT#), 95, 109
less than, 31
line graph, 129
line numbers, 41
listing, 123
LISTO7, 14
LOAD, 78
local variables, 41, 53
loop, 123

machine code, 123
meaningful variables, 11
megabyte, 123
menu, 10, 34, 114, 123
menu–driven programs, 9, 61
MID$, 27
MODE, 17
modem, 123
modifying a file, 102
modular design, 9
module, 69

Network, 123

ON ERROR..., 37, 66, 112
opening printer, 62
OPENIN, 81, 117
OPENOUT, 80, 97
OPENUP, 97, 109, 117
*OPT 4,3, 119
output, 8

Padding (a field), 107
parameter passing, 53
percentage, 39
peripherals, 124

PI, 139
pie chart, 138
PLOT, 137
pointer, 77, 80, 93, 102
"PRESS SPACE", 19
PRINT, 19
PRINT#, 80, 83
procedure, 10, 20, 34, 69, 124
processing, 7
program design, 8
programming strategy, 92
PTR#, 92, 93, 98, 116

QWERTY, 124

RAM, 124
random access file, 76, 80, 92, 116
reading a file, 81, 83
record, 14, 99, 105, 113, 124
redefining origin (VDU 29), 130
RENUMBER, 41
REPEAT...UNTIL..., 11, 12, 13, 34, 87, 115
REPORT, 117
RIGHT$, 27
ROM, 124

SAVE, 78
scales, 131
searching, 22, 125
sector, 77, 108, 140
sequential file, 76, 80
Shell sort, 55
software, 125
sort time, 51
sorting, 44, 125
source file, 88
speed (of program), 30, 51
string variables, 15, 125, 121
STRING$, 107, 115
structured programs, 8, 125
subroutine, 125
subscript, 125
swap routine, 45, 63
syntax error, 126

TAB, 19
terminator (of data), 126
text file, 126
TIME, 51
time delay, 19
top-down programming, 9
tracks, 77
truncating (a field), 107
*TYPE, 126

Update, 19, 83, 102

VAL, 15, 19, 36, 127
variable names, 11, 13, 127
VDU, 127
VDU2, VDU3, 62

Winchester hard disk, 7, 110, 123
word processing, 127
writing to a file, 80

x,y co-ordinates, 131